The Thirteenth Apostle

The Thirteenth Apostle

What the Gospel of Judas Really Says

April D. DeConick

continuum

Published by Continuum
The Tower Building,
11 York Road,
London SE1 7NX

80 Maiden Lane,
Suite 704,
New York, NY 10038

www.continuumbooks.com

ISBN-10: HB: 0-8264-9964-3
ISBN-13: HB: 978-0-8264-9964-6

British Library Cataloguing-in-Publication Data
A catalogue record for this book is available from the British Library.

Typeset by BookEns Ltd, Royston, Herts.
Printed and bound in the U.S.A.

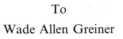

To
Wade Allen Greiner

Contents

List of Figures ix

Timeline xiv

Preface xvii

PART 1   An Unfamiliar Story

CHAPTER 1   The Silenced Voice   3

CHAPTER 2   A Gnostic Catechism   22

PART 2   Translation Matters

CHAPTER 3   A Mistaken Gospel   45

CHAPTER 4   The *Gospel of Judas* in English Translation   62

PART 3   Good Old Judas?

CHAPTER 5   Judas the Confessor   95

CHAPTER 6   Judas the Demon   109

CHAPTER 7   Judas the Sacrificer   125

CHAPTER 8   An Ancient Gnostic Parody   140

Epilogue   148

Appendix 1:   Further Reading   155

Appendix 2:   A Synopsis of Sethian Gnostic Literature   167

Appendix 3:   Testimony from the Church Fathers on the *Gospel of Judas*   174

Appendix 4:   Q&A with April Deconick   178

Notes   183

Index of Authors   195

Index of References   197

List of Figures

Fig. 1   The Nile Valley in second century CE   x

Fig. 2   The Roman World at the time of Irenaeus
          c. 180 CE   xi

Fig. 3   The Roman World at the time of Constantine
          c. 325 CE   xii

Fig. 4   The Ptolemaic Universe   26

Fig. 5   The Sethian Godhead   36

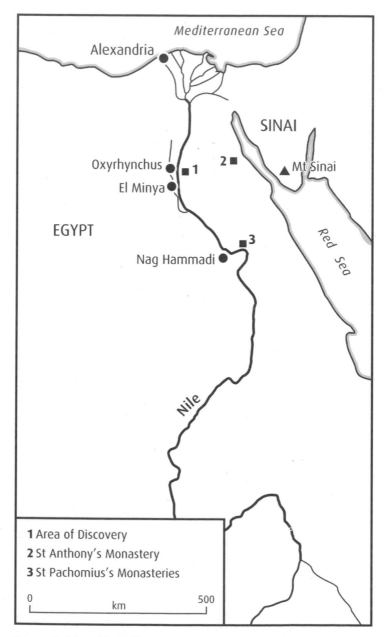

Figure 1. The Nile Valley in second century CE

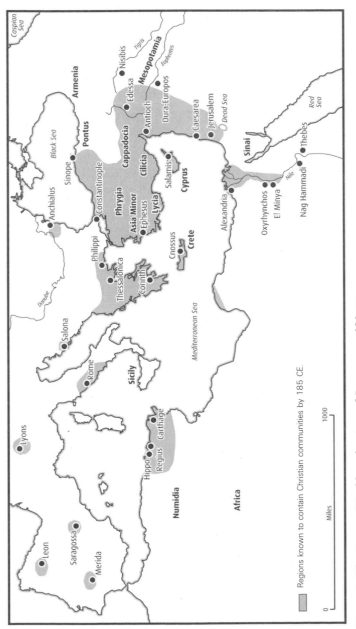

Figure 2. *The Roman World at the time of Irenaeus c. 180 CE*

Regions known to contain Christian communities by 185 CE.

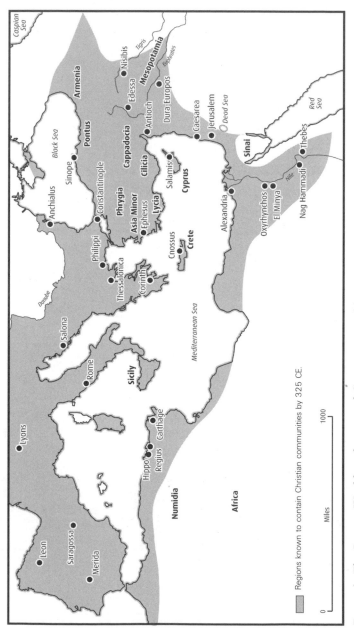

Figure 3. The Roman World at the time of Constantine c. 325 CE

Regions known to contain Christian communities by 325 CE.

New Testament and Sethian Gnostic Texts

49–62 CE
Paul's letters written
60–90 CE
Gospels of Mark, Matthew, and Luke written and Acts

90–100 CE
Gospel of John and Revelation written
100–125 CE
Sophia of Jesus Christ written
125–130 CE
Pastoral and Catholic Epistles, *Apocryphon of John,* and *Trimorphic Protennoia* written

150 CE
Gospel of Judas, Apocalypse of Adam, Hypostasis of the Archons, and *Thought of Norea* written
150–200 CE
Paul's letters and Gospels of Mark, Matthew, Luke, and John begin to gain scriptural status
175–200 CE
Holy Book of the Great Invisible Spirit, Thunder, and *Melchizedek* written
180 CE
Bishop Irenaeus writes about *Gospel of Judas*

| 1 CE |
| 100 CE |

Early Christian History

30 CE
Jesus crucified

70 CE
Jewish Temple destroyed
80–130 CE
Rise of Gnostic lodges

100–150 CE
Ebionite church forms; Marcionite church forms
118–136 CE
Valentinus teaches in Alexandria
132–135 CE
Basilides teaches in Alexandria
138 CE
Valentinus moves to Rome
140 CE
Valentinus loses election to Pius I

155–160 CE
Justin Martyr writing in Rome
172 CE
Failed apocalyptic prediction of Church of New Prophecy

200 CE

200–225 CE
Second Treatise of the Great Seth, Zostrianos, Allogenes, Fragment of Allogenes, and *Three Steles of Seth* written

200 CE
Tertullian writes in support of apostolic succession
220–240 CE
Origen creates the Devil-Ransom theology
225 CE
Pseudo-Tertullian writes

300 CE

275–300 CE
Marsanes written
280–325 CE
Untitled Treatise written
300–350 CE
Coptic manuscripts of the Tchacos Codex and the Nag Hammadi codices copied

275–325 CE
Apostolic Christianity becoming dominant

325 CE
Council of Nicaea

400 CE

367 CE
Bishop Athanasius writes first list of 27 books of New Testament
375 CE
Bishop Epiphanius condemns *Gospel of Judas*

380 CE
Christianity becomes the official religion of Roman Empire

Preface

I did not write this book because I wanted to. I wrote this book because I felt I had to. I have very mixed feelings about publishing it because I do not want my criticisms to detract from the absolutely outstanding work and dedication of the National Geographic team in restoring an old manuscript that was in such a state of deterioration that the deciphering of any page was practically hopeless. I could never have done what they did – piecing together the fragments of the manuscript with tweezers. Their use of computer technology was brilliant, working with computer scanning techniques to help put the bits and pieces back together again. From a situation of hopelessness, we now have 85 per cent of the original *Gospel of Judas* restored! For this, I am forever thankful to Professors Rodolphe Kasser, Gregor Wurst, Marvin Meyer, and François Gaudard.

However, when my own English translation of the Coptic transcription and interpretation of the *Gospel of Judas* began to deviate substantially from theirs, I became worried and troubled. The first scholar I corresponded with about these discrepancies was Professor Wolf-Peter Funk from the University of Laval, soon after the *Gospel of Judas* was released by National Geographic in April 2006. Although our exchange consisted of only a couple of brief e-mails, it was Professor Funk who encouraged me to pursue the trajectory that my project had begun to take. His correspondence gave me the initial courage to follow through systematically with my contrary interpretation of Judas and his Gospel. For this, I owe Professor Funk a great debt.

By early October 2006, I had completed my initial interpretation and analysis of the text. I flew to Eisenach, Germany, to participate in a conference on the *Gospel of Thomas*. Professor Stephen Emmel was in attendance and graciously took the time to hear the ideas I was forming about the *Gospel of Judas* and share some of his own thoughts. My thanks to him for these inspiring conversations.

A couple of weeks later, on October 27 and 28, Professor Madeleine Scopello from the University of Paris at the Sorbonne hosted a conference on the *Gospel of Judas*. All of the papers presented at the Sorbonne conference will be published in 2008 in a collection edited by her, in the Nag Hammadi and Manichaean Studies series.[1] Her colloquium showcased an international body of scholars who had gathered to discuss their initial readings of this newly recovered and reconstructed text from the Tchacos Codex. There was a sense of relief that those of us in the academic "Gnostic" community could finally discuss openly a Gospel we had only heard about in private whispers, since the team selected by National Geographic to work on the text had been required to sign non-disclosure agreements.

I am extremely grateful to Madeleine Scopello for hosting such an outstanding conference, and for inviting me to participate. I doubt I would have gained the courage to write this book had it not been for my involvement in that conference. It was there that I realized I was not alone in my reading of the *Gospel of Judas* nor in my criticism of the translation published by National Geographic. There were several scholars who had independently come to the same conclusions, presenting papers with very similar interpretations and criticisms of the National Geographic transcription, translation, and representation of the Gospel. I am very thankful to Professor Stephen Emmel, Professor John Turner, and Professor

Louis Painchaud for sharing with me their perspectives and written
academic analyses of the *Gospel of Judas*. My own work has
matured as a result of our interactions and their support.

Professor Stephen Emmel offered a paper (read in *abstentia*)
entitled "The Presuppositions and the Purpose of the *Gospel of
Judas*." The paper questioned whether or not the *Gospel of Judas*
understands Judas' sacrifice as a favored deed. Professor Emmel
argues for the likelihood that the translation of the Coptic on p. 56,
ll. 17–21 is a prediction that Judas will do the *worst* thing of all by
sacrificing Jesus, rather than the best thing of all as the National
Geographic translation implies.

Equally outstanding was Professor Painchaud's pioneering
contribution, "Polemical Aspects of the *Gospel of Judas*," which so
pointedly describes the irony in this Gospel, and its hostility toward
certain Christian beliefs, particularly those beliefs that perpetuate
cultic sacrifice. Professor Painchaud spoke at length about how the
Gospel of Judas aggressively opposes a form of mainstream
Christianity in the second century that it associates with the
"twelve apostles," over whom Judas reigns.

I found particularly stimulating the brilliant and systematic
analysis presented by Professor John Turner, "The Place of the
Gospel of Judas in Sethian Tradition." In his paper, he has done a
stunning job of offering alternative reconstructions to damaged
areas of the Gospel. I have become completely dependent on his
reconstruction of 52.5–8, since the National Geographic reconstruction of this area of the manuscript, particularly the names
"Seth" and "Christ," is not compatible with the mythology of the
Gospel. Professor Turner offers a much more reasonable reconstruction given the mythological content, and so I have chosen to
go with his Coptic reconstruction at this point in the manuscript
and deviate from the transcription made by National Geographic.

The same is true of 51.1, where I rely on his reconstruction, preferring "Eleleth" to "El."

I am also indebted to Professor Einar Thomassen for sharing with me a copy of his paper, "Is Judas Really the Hero of the Gospel?," presented on November 10, 2006, at the University of Chicago. John Turner was in attendance and enthusiastically recommended that I contact Professor Thomassen. I found Thomassen's cogent remarks to be so compatible with my own independent analysis of the *Gospel of Judas* that I was stunned. His narrative analysis is compelling.

My own academic contribution to the Sorbonne conference was a presentation entitled "The Mystery of Judas' Betrayal: What the *Gospel of Judas* Really Says." It became my "think tank" and subtitle for *The Thirteenth Apostle: What the Gospel of Judas Really Says*. The ideas I developed in that academic paper are the ideas that form the basis of *The Thirteenth Apostle*. I will remember with fondness Professor Marvin Meyer's reaction to my presentation. He was the first to raise his hand and ask me a series of tough questions. And after our discussion, we went out to dinner and laughed as friends do.

Many have helped me with this book, and I would like to extend my thanks to them. Mr Haaris Naqvi, my editor from Continuum, has gone above and beyond for me with this book, devoting not only time and precision, but also his own intellectual and artistic input. Professor John Turner read this book in proof and gave me very helpful feedback. While I was writing *The Thirteenth Apostle*, two students came to study with me from abroad as they wrote portions of their dissertations. Each of these students, Mr Matteo Grosso and Rev Judy Redman, read the book in manuscript and offered their editorial advice as well as their encouragement.

This book is dedicated to my husband, Wade Allen Greiner, who watched the National Geographic documentary with me. He was there when I first said, "Oh no, something is really wrong," and has been listening to me ever since.

April D. DeConick
Third Sunday of Lent
First Scrutiny of the Elect
March 11, 2007

PART 1

An Unfamiliar Story

CHAPTER 1

The Silenced Voice

When I first read the *Gospel of Judas* in English translation, I didn't like it. Jesus was rude. He laughed inappropriately. He treated his twelve disciples as enemies. And Judas Iscariot was the only one who knew anything.

I couldn't help but think about Bishop Irenaeus of Lyons' description of this old Gnostic Gospel as a "fictitious history." Writing in the late second century about the *Gospel of Judas*, Irenaeus says that the central character is "Judas the traitor," who alone knew "the truth as none of the others did." Because of his special knowledge, he "accomplished the mystery of the betrayal" which threw the cosmos into chaos. He links the *Gospel of Judas* with certain Gnostics who thought that all the evil people in the biblical stories – Cain, Esau, Korah, the Sodomites – were their ancestors.[1]

Now I have always been suspicious of Irenaeus' description of the *Gospel of Judas*, especially the evil pedigree he links it to, since he was writing to discredit the Gnostics and suppress one of their Gospels. But I think my initial reaction to reading the *Gospel of Judas* was probably similar to his. I didn't like the unfamiliar story.

Then I watched the documentary, "The *Gospel of Judas*: The Lost Version of Christ's Betrayal," premièred on the National Geographic Channel.[2] I quickly became intrigued by the fantastic and exciting interpretation set out by the National Geographic team of scholars, an interpretation where Judas was Jesus' best friend and collaborator.[3] The National Geographic interpretation sounded like something from Martin Scorsese's movie *The Last Temptation of Christ*. A Gnostic Judas? Could it be?

So, even though I had no intention of writing about the *Gospel of Judas* (I was in the middle of writing a book on another early Christian Gospel and didn't need or want the distraction), I eagerly went to the National Geographic website. From that website, I downloaded their English translation as well as their transcription of the *Gospel of Judas* in its original language, Coptic, which is an old form of Egyptian written with Greek letters.[4] I spent a few days in my office between classes translating the *Gospel of Judas*, searching for the sublime Judas who was supposed to be there.

I didn't find the sublime Judas, at least not in Coptic. What I found were a series of translation choices made by the National Geographic team, choices that permitted a Judas to emerge in the English translation who was different from the Judas in the Coptic original. In the original, Judas was not only *not* sublime, he was far more demonic than any Judas I know in any other piece of early Christian literature, Gnostic or otherwise.

I found this both fascinating and frustrating. But more importantly, I felt misled. The *Gospel of Judas* we had learned about from the National Geographic publications and productions simply does not exist.[5] It isn't a Gospel about a "good" Judas, or even a "poor old" Judas. It is a Gospel parody about a "demon" Judas written by a particular group of Gnostic Christians known as the Sethians who lived in the second century CE.

The purpose of the *Gospel of Judas* was to criticize "mainstream" or "apostolic" Christianity from the point of view of the Sethian Gnostics. The Sethian Christians, whose religious beliefs I will describe in detail in the next chapter, were involved in an intra-religious debate that was raging in the second century as a number of distinct Christianities struggled for control of Christianity. Christianity in the second century was not controlled by a single church or a single hierarchy or a single orthodoxy. In fact, "orthodoxy" (correct thinking and practice) and "heresy" (wrong thinking and practice) were very relative terms. Who was orthodox and who was a heretic depended upon where you were standing. If you were a mainstream or apostolic Christian, you were orthodox and everyone else was a heretic. If you were a Sethian Gnostic Christian, you were orthodox and everyone else was a heretic.

So the barbs in the *Gospel of Judas* are many, all directed at the theology and practices of apostolic Christians. The *Gospel of Judas* attempts to harpoon apostolic Christianity for its blind reliance on the authority of the twelve apostles for its teachings. For the Sethian Gnostics, truth can only be had through revelation, through a personal religious experience of God. So external authorities beware. The Sethians who wrote the *Gospel of Judas* especially found atonement theology unconscionable. Apostolic Christianity had long defended Jesus' death as a necessary sacrifice made to God the Father for the purpose of atonement, vicariously redeeming humanity from its sins. The Sethian Gnostics found this doctrine morally reprehensible – no different from child sacrifice or murder – and thus not an action that could be condoned by God. The *Gospel of Judas* is fascinating in this respect, building a very sophisticated response to skewer the atonement. And the one figure that they use to do this is the cursed Judas Iscariot, the demon who was responsible for Jesus' death.

So Christianity in the second century was sectarian and in conflict. Christianity was only in its youth. It hadn't figured itself out yet. It was trying to determine its relationship with Judaism, its understanding of Jesus, its view of salvation, its use of rituals, its hierarchy, its position on women, its sacred scripture, its interpretation of that scripture, and so forth. For every one of these issues, there were several answers among Christians. And many of these Christians formed their own communities. They talked to each other. They argued with each other. They agreed and they disagreed. Sometimes the discussions became heated, turned nasty, included name-calling, false accusations, and real hatred and bitterness.

It is within this complicated and confrontational environment that the *Gospel of Judas* was written. For this reason, it is necessary for us to become somewhat familiar with the general landscape of second-century Christianity. Who were the apostolic Christians? What faith were they defending? What other forms of Christianity existed? What were the disputes all about?

The Apostolic Church

The form of second-century Christianity that looks most like Christianity today is what various scholars call "proto-orthodox," "mainstream," "catholic," or "apostolic" Christianity, although I must point out that it wasn't the same as Christianity today. It would take two more centuries before the apostolic churches would sort out their major theological tenets, including Jesus' relationship to God (was he the same as God or subordinate to God?), the problem of Christ's two natures (how was his divine nature related to his human nature?), and the Trinity (how were the Father, the Son, and the Holy Spirit the same God and yet distinguishable?). The same can be said regarding their rituals. In the late fourth and early fifth centuries, Augustine of Hippo was still trying to sort out whether a person needed to be rebaptized if a lapsed priest had initially performed the baptism, and whether infant baptism was to be preferred over adult baptism.

Apostolic Christianity's main rituals were the initiation rites (water baptism and anointing) and a sacred meal of thanksgiving, when the bread and the cup were shared in remembrance of Jesus' death (the eucharist). It is a form of Christianity that was lauded by many men in the ancient world who were powerful bishops and respected theologians. They have become known as the "Church Fathers."

One of the things that these men agreed on was a basic formulation of their faith, a formulation which they claimed was passed down to them from the twelve apostles. An early form of the Apostolic Creed recorded by Irenaeus contains elements of the faith that would become the normative expression of Christianity – belief in one God, the creator of the universe; his Son Jesus Christ, who was born of the flesh of the Virgin Mary, who was crucified and raised from the dead, who ascended into heaven, and who will return at the end of the world to resurrect in the flesh the dead, judging everyone, punishing the wicked with damnation and rewarding the righteous with life everlasting:

> For the Church, though dispersed throughout the whole world, even to the ends of the earth, has received from the apostles and their disciples this faith: in one God, the Father Almighty, who made the heaven and the earth and the seas and all things that are in them; and in one Christ Jesus, the Son of God, who became incarnate for our salvation; and in the Holy Spirit, who proclaimed through the prophets the dispensations and the advents, and the birth from a virgin, and the passion, and the resurrection from the dead, and the incarnate ascension into heaven of the beloved Christ Jesus, our Lord, and his future manifestation from heaven in the glory of the Father to sum up all things, and to raise up anew all flesh of the whole human race,

in order that to Christ Jesus, our Lord and God and Savior and King, according to the will of the invisible Father, every knee should bow, of things in heaven, and things in earth, and things under the earth, and that every tongue should confess to him, and that he should execute just judgment towards all; that he may send spiritual wickedness and the angels who transgressed and came into a state of rebellion together with the ungodly, and unrighteous, and wicked, and profane among men, into the everlasting fire; but may, as an act of grace, confer immortality on the righteous and holy, and those who have kept his commandments, and have persevered in his love, some from the beginning, and others from their repentance, and may surround them with everlasting glory.[6]

In the discussion following his record of this creed, Irenaeus makes several assertions to justify it. He says that although Christianity is scattered "throughout the whole world," her "one house carefully preserves" this faith in many parts of the world. He emphasizes that this faith is "traditional" and "one." He then goes on to declare that all forms of Christianity which deviate from this faith are "blasphemy." He compares the deviant Christians to Satan's fallen angels, "apostates" or renegades who will be punished by God for their wickedness and deceit.[7]

Of course, his assertions are rhetorical, meant to gain the upper hand in the debate about what shape Christianity should take. The creed that he lauds as "old" from the time of the apostles, in fact came into existence in the second century as a weapon in the arsenal against Christians whose Christianity looked very different from Irenaeus'. If there was a "traditional" or "old" creed from the apostles, it would have been close to what Paul remembers when he tells us that he passed on to his churches the traditional teaching that he likely received from the Jerusalem church, "that Christ died for our sins in accordance with the scriptures, that he was buried, that he was raised on the third day in accordance with the scriptures."[8]

The perception that apostolic Christianity was the dominant or major form of Christianity in the second century is only a perception, not a historical reality. It is a false impression that results from the fact that the surviving literature survived because it supported the form of Christianity that came to dominate and suppress all others. The emergence of orthodoxy from apostolic Christianity was a complicated process, involving a web of factors, not the least of which was a Roman emperor, Constantine, who wanted a single agreed faith.

One of the strategies used by the apostolic churches when they began to emerge as the orthodox tradition was to burn the books of those they declared to be heretics. This leaves history with the impression that their own writings were the dominant writings or expressed the opinions of the overwhelming majority, while other Christians had little or nothing to say. Of course, this is not true, but it means that historians have a difficult task trying to reconstruct the other forms of Christianity from the charred remains. Thank goodness that the apostolic Christians were argumentative and critical of other forms of Christianity, because their pens left traces of the suppressed Christianities. The greatest joy for the historian of early Christianity, however, is the accidents of history that have preserved some of the writings from those suppressed forms of Christianity, like the recent discovery of the *Gospel of Judas*.

The Marcionite Church

So who were these second-century apostolic creeds targeting? There were a number of other sectarian groups that were widespread and powerful. Perhaps the largest and most influential sectarian church was the one established by Marcion, a Christian from Asia Minor. He was born in 85 CE in the city of Sinope on the shore of the Black Sea. In the early part of the second century, he traveled to Rome, where he joined the local church and planned to study as a Christian theologian. It took Marcion several years to work out his systematic theology and write two major books laying out his system.

He was a very astute biblical scholar, who loved Paul's letters and knew the Jewish scriptures inside out. During the course of his rigorous study and criticism of the Jewish scriptures, he noticed that the God of the Jewish scriptures was wrathful, vengeful, and jealous, the opposite of the God of mercy, grace, and love that Jesus and Paul proclaimed. So Marcion thought that the Unknown God that Paul preached about in Acts to the Athenians was Jesus' Father, the Christian God, while Yahweh was the wrathful God of the Jews.

This distinction made sense to him in light of Paul's discussion about the Jewish Law and the advent of Jesus. Marcion took Paul's thought to its radical and logical conclusion – if Christ brought an end to the Jewish Law, then Judaism had been severed from Christianity. Marcion understood the Jewish Law to contain unnecessary and arbitrary commandments, which resulted in punishment and death. That law may be applicable to the Jews, whose God is Yahweh, but it made no sense to the Christians, whose God was the Unknown God of mercy, grace, and love proclaimed by Jesus and Paul. These thoughts led him to the conclusion that Christians needed to repudiate the Jewish scriptures and replace them with a New Testament, a Christian scripture that would include the Gospel of Luke and ten of Paul's letters.

Once Marcion had completed his critical analysis of the scriptures, he called a meeting, inviting a number of Christian elders from the church in Rome. He presented his systematic theology of two Gods and two faiths to them, challenging them to debate. They weren't impressed. They returned to him all monies he had donated to their church and threw him out.

So Marcion went home. But he was not defeated. Instead, he became an active Christian missionary, establishing Marcionite churches everywhere he went. Justin Martyr, writing in Rome in the middle of the second century, complains that Marcion was successfully teaching his views to "many people of every nation."[9] Fifty years later Tertullian of Carthage wrote, "Marcion's heretical tradition has filled the whole world."[10] His churches formed the bedrock of the Christian tradition in many regions of Asia Minor, representing the original form of Christianity in some of these locales. Later orthodox church leaders like Bishop Cyril of Jerusalem (350 CE) had to warn travelers to be cautious about attending church services in an unknown village. It could be a Marcionite church they had wandered into.[11] There are even Arabic reports of Marcionite congregations in the East as late as the tenth century![12] The success and longevity of the Marcionite tradition can be measured in terms of the huge efforts that other Christian leaders expended in writing polemic against them. Around 200 CE, Tertullian alone devoted five books to this purpose.

The Ebionite Church

At the opposite end of the spectrum was the Ebionite church. This was the Jewish Christian church most widespread in eastern Syria. The writings which preserve many of their traditions are called the *Pseudo-Clementines* (200 CE). They appear to have had their own version of the Gospel of Matthew, likely an Aramaic translation of the Greek original with midrashic flourishes. The name of these Christians is to be traced back to the Hebrew word for " the poor," *ebyon*. They took seriously the ethic of poverty that had been the foundation of Jesus' movement.

They are described by the Church Fathers as Jews who remained faithful to the Jewish Law, while also honoring Jesus.[13] They believed, as the Jewish faith taught, in one God, and in the Jewish scriptures as revealed by the one God. They did not believe that Jesus was born from a virgin. In fact, their version of Matthew did not have the first two chapters. Jesus was the natural son of Joseph and Mary, chosen by God to be his prophet. At his baptism, the Holy Spirit entered Jesus, and at his death it left him.

Jesus' job while on earth was to be the voice of God, instructing his followers how to live righteously according to the "original" Jewish Law. The Ebionites thought that the Jewish scripture had become corrupted over time by the interpolation of human opinion and erroneous judgments, including concessions from Moses himself. So Jesus, the True Prophet, was to point out the false messages corrupting the scripture, while teaching the original intent of the Jewish Law given by God to Moses on Mount Sinai. The false passages included all references to God as a humanlike being with emotions or a body, all plural references to God ("us," "we," "our"), all references to the sacrificial Temple cult. The Ebionites, in the wake of the destruction of the Temple in 70 CE, began to teach that Jesus had come to abolish all sacrifices.

As for their practices, they used baptism as their initiation ritual, which they thought cleansed the convert from his or her sinful past. Daily baths were used to keep themselves in a state of holiness. They circumcised their children and lived their life in observance of the "corrected" Mosaic Law. They worshiped on the Sabbath (Saturday) as well as the Lord's Day (Sunday), and also kept the Jewish holidays. Particularly important to them was the celebration of Passover every year. They maintained a restrictive table fellowship. As Jews they refused to eat meals or even have conversations with other Christians, whom they considered to be Gentiles. As for Paul, the apostle to the Gentiles, he was loathed. They taught that his letters should be rejected by Christians. They called Paul the "Apostate," the renegade from the Law.

The evidence suggests that they are the remnant of the form of Christianity original to Jerusalem, when James the brother of Jesus and the twelve apostles first established a church after Jesus' death. But this Jewish form of Christianity did not take root in most parts of the Mediterranean world, where Gentiles dominated in terms of converts. One of the paradoxes of Christianity's growth among the Gentiles and its deviant interpretation of the Jewish scriptures was its separation from the religion that gave it birth. So by the second century, the Ebionites, who carried on a version of the earliest form of Christianity, had become a small church dissimilar to the majority of other Christian churches. Justin Martyr from Rome wasn't sure how to react to them. He thought it probably best for Christians to try to get along with them as "brothers," as long as the Ebionites didn't try to force the rest of the Christian population to follow the Jewish Law and didn't refuse to eat at the same table with them.[14]

The Church of New Prophecy

The New Prophecy movement, also known as Montanism, was quite different from the ones I have so far described. It was a protest movement, wishing to reclaim the original form of Christianity, its prophetic and charismatic roots. Three Christian prophets were the leaders of this reform movement: a man named Montanus, and two women, Priscilla and Maximilla. Montanus was from a village called Pepuza in a province in Asia Minor known as Phrygia, and this is where their movement was centered. These three prophets knew the Gospel of John and the book of Revelation, although they also wrote books of their own, based on their revelations. Only a smattering of their prophetic sayings has come down to us.

What were they protesting against? The secularization of the apostolic churches. Their aim was to restore Christianity to its original form as a religion ruled by the Holy Spirit and focused on the coming of the end of the world. The two women were considered to be the main prophets of the movement, the principal voices of the Holy Spirit. They claimed to be inspired by the "Paraclete," the name for the Holy Spirit found in the Gospel of John. Montanus himself claimed to be a manifestation of the Paraclete, whom Jesus had promised to send to the disciples after his death.[15] His role as the manifestation of the Paraclete was to lead everyone to the Truth.[16]

The women's claim to be prophets is particularly illuminating given the fact that Montanism was a protest and reform movement. Our earliest records from Paul indicate that one of the offices within the oldest churches was that of the prophet. This was an office that women filled, as well as men.[17] But as the apostolic churches became more secularized, they shut women out of their traditional roles as prophets and leaders. So the New Prophecy movement reclaimed for women their leadership roles in prophetic offices.

Priscilla made particular prophecies about the end of the world that included the descent of Jerusalem from heaven to a specific hill she had identified in Phrygia, a prophecy based in part on the book of Revelation.[18] She speculated about the date of its arrival, using references from Genesis 6.3 and 8.1–5 to predict its descent in the year 172 CE to the mountain where Noah's ark was believed to have come to rest. Once New Jerusalem descended upon this Phyrgian hill, she claimed, a thousand-year reign of Christ would be established on earth.

So the Montanist prophets called out to Christians everywhere to set up a camp at the bottom of this hill and await the arrival of the new Jerusalem. Here, they thought, true Christianity would be established, ready for the coming of Christ's reign. In camp, the ethics were rigid. A strict code of asceticism was adopted to prepare for the great day. Wasn't it the 144,000 virgins who would be redeemed?[19] So celibacy was practically demanded even within marriage, and second marriage completely forbidden. Rigorous fasting for one day a week was required and a diet of dry foods encouraged. The reason for the dry diet had to do with ancient physiology. The ancients believed that reducing fluids by mouth would decrease fluids that needed to be excreted not only as urine, but also as semen. So the dry diet was used to control sexual urges and encourage celibacy. Absolution of sin after baptism was completely refused, and penance for sins was severe. Martyrdom was encouraged because persecution was predicted as a sign of the end in Revelation, a book which also taught that the believer should die for his or her faith.

This apocalyptic movement was highly successful. The records of the Church Fathers indicate that Christians abandoned their families, their work, and their property to come and camp out at the base of the mountain. Of course the movement failed and everyone went home once it was evident that the new Jerusalem wasn't going to descend on the mountain. However, the movement didn't die out; it turned into a church which continued for centuries. The Church of New Prophecy was able to survive and flourish because its members became door-to-door itinerant preachers. They weren't embarrassed by the failure of the prophecy. They just admitted that their calculations for the Last Day were wrong, and then they intensified their propaganda.

In this way they offered a rigorous and charismatic alternative to the apostolic Christian church, which was being criticized for loosening its standards on mandatory fasting and marriage. The Church of New Prophecy spread beyond Asia Minor, to Rome, Gaul, Syria, Thrace, and North Africa. We have a story in the Syrian traditions about John of Ephesus who, in the sixth century, apparently had had enough of them. He went to the main Montanist church in Pepuza and burnt the church to the ground along with the bones of the prophets Montanus, Maximilla, and Priscilla which were housed there, and the books they had written.[20]

One of the most famous converts to the Church of New Prophecy was Tertullian, who is also famous for being one of the leading theologians within the Roman Catholic Church in the West. He was one of the early framers of Trinitarian thought and many of his ideas about the human and divine natures of Christ became the basis for western contributions to the Christological debate. Tertullian was attracted to the strict ethics of the Church of New Prophecy, as well as the strength of its Christians, who not only were willing to die grisly deaths as martyrs for the faith, but actually did so. Some of these deaths are recorded in the *Martyrdom of Perpetua and Felicity*. It appears that the Bishop of Rome was also impressed. Tertullian writes that the Bishop had "acknowledged the prophetic gifts of Montanus, Prisca [or: Priscilla], and Maximilla" and had "bestowed his peace on the churches of Asia and Phrygia." Later, though, Tertullian complains that the Bishop was persuaded by false accusations lodged against the prophets and their churches, and so turned against them. In anger, Tertullian says that the Paraclete was "put to flight" in Rome.[21]

The Gnostics

Perhaps the second-century Christians most difficult to describe are the "Gnostics" or "Knowers." The difficulty lies in the fact that they do not represent one group or one church. As we will see in the next chapter, there was no separate Gnostic church. Rather, these people formed lodges or seminaries where they would gather for instruction and initiation into God's mysteries. Some Gnostic groups identified more closely with apostolic churches than others, attending them on Sundays in addition to their lodge activities. Other Gnostic groups turned away from formal Christian worship altogether, and only attended lodge. Of the numerous Gnostic groups in the second century, three serve as good examples of the range of relationships Gnostic Christians had with apostolic Christians.

The Valentinian Gnostics called themselves "Christians." The Valentinian author of the *Gospel of Philip* said, "When we were Hebrews, we were orphans and had only our mother, but when we became Christians we had both father and mother."[22] They appear to have been closely tied to the apostolic churches, attending them

regularly. In addition to these ordinary church services, the
Valentinian Gnostics met as a "secret society" or a closed seminary
circle. They formed conventicles led by famous Valentinian
theologians – Valentinus, Theodotus, Marcus, Heracleon, and
Ptolemy.

Valentinians held their rituals (baptism, anointing, eucharist)
in common with the apostolic churches, although their interpretation of the effects of those rituals was unique to them. All rituals,
they believed, had an esoteric purpose unknown to ordinary
Christians. In addition they probably used further practices for
initiation ceremonies in the Gnostic conventicle itself, but exactly
what those were has yet to be fully recovered from the texts. It is
likely that a second baptism was required. What this means is that
the Valentinians straddled the fence. They fully participated in the
rituals of the apostolic churches, which they attended regularly. At
the same time, they engaged in ritual activities in their lodges or
seminaries, which were for them an additional but separate sphere
of communal worship. The modern example most comparable to
the Valentinians might be Christians who also belong to the Mason
Lodge or the ecumenical Bible study club.

Some scholars have suggested that the Valentinians engaged in
a special sexual initiation ritual called the "Bridal Chamber." But
this is a misreading of the Valentinian traditions. The Valentinians
believed that monogamous marriage is to be respected as a
sacrament, that love-making must involve a prayerful (rather than
lustful) orientation because it is a reflection of the eternal marriages
between God's own male and female aspects. Love-making is also
the procreative moment, so the Valentinians were also very
concerned to maintain a prayerful orientation so that the children
they conceived would contain within them a strong spirit rather
than a weak one. Human marriage, they thought, anticipated an

end-of-the-world event known as the Bridal Chamber. At that final eschatological moment, all the perfected human spirits would marry angels. Together, the couples would enter the Godhead, which would become for them a bridal chamber. This vision of the end of time is a vision of mystical reunion with God, a sacred marriage between the human spirit and the great Father.

Valentinians believed that all Christians (Gnostic and apostolic) would be saved, although how this was accomplished depended on whether you were an initiated Gnostic Christian or not. Their interpretation of Jewish and Christian scripture tended to be allegorical, rather than subversive. They taught a distinctive Gnostic mythology with a creator god who would be redeemed by Jesus, rather than conquered. Many features of their beliefs are very close to those of the apostolic church. It is not always easy to separate their theology from Alexandrian Fathers like Origen. So closely were they tied to the apostolic churches that Valentinus himself was nominated in the election of the Bishop of Rome in the mid-second century and was only narrowly defeated.

The Basilidian Gnostics, however, expressed a different self-identification: "We are no longer Jews and not yet Christians." These Gnostics understood themselves to be outside the apostolic churches, although they do not appear to have harbored animosity toward them. Like the Valentinians, they formed conventicles, but unlike the Valentinians, the Basilidians were not connected to the worship houses of the apostolic Christians. They worshiped separately. One of the interesting fragments about the Basilidians reports that they observed their own liturgical calendar, celebrating Jesus' baptism (January 6th) in vigil the night of the 5th and reading scriptures.[23] This means that they are the first recorded Christians to have celebrated the festival we call today the "Epiphany of our Lord." These Gnostics appear to have congregrated in a seminary circle or lodge, taught by Basilides himself or one of his students. Basilides was a famous Christian philosopher in his day, and wrote the first commentaries on some of the texts that later would become part of the New Testament.

The Basilidians had a very extensive cosmology that included 365 heavens, one for every day of the year. All were populated by numerous powers and angels whose names the initiate had to learn. The chief of these powers was Abrasax, whose name in Greek letters has the numerical value 365, although the name "Abrasax" appears to be of Semitic origin, a secret paraphrase of one of the Jewish names for God. Basilides taught a variety of determinism that he got from reading Paul: that only a few (the Gnostics) are chosen to be saved. The rest of humanity would be destroyed at the end when God's original intended order would be re-established. Christ came to liberate the elect from the grip of Abrasax and the world order he had erroneously set up. Salvation is for the soul alone, not the body, which is the creation of the powers that rule this world.

The most confrontational Gnostics appear to have been the Sethian Christians, those responsible for writing the *Gospel of Judas*. In the next chapter, I will describe their form of Gnostic Christianity in detail in order to give a full context for the religiosity of the *Gospel of Judas*. They understood themselves to be Gnostic Christians, the only type of Christian who could understand Jesus' message. They were completely opposed to apostolic Christianity and did not consider the apostolic Christians to be real Christians.

So in the *Gospel of Judas*, we will find our familiar story turned upside down. Jesus mocks and criticizes the apostolic twelve, who are characterized as faithless and ignorant. Jesus' voice is the Gnostic voice challenging the apostolic Christians to reassess their faith, to listen to their own reason and consciences rather than blindly accept their faith because they thought it was handed down to them from the Twelve.

The *Gospel of Judas* has grown on me. It has taken me in. Studying the text in Coptic has made me change my mind about it and appreciate its bitter voice, a voice that was marginalized and then silenced for almost two thousand years. The *Gospel of Judas* is a very sophisticated Gospel written from a perspective we are not often exposed to – from the perspective of a Gnostic Christian in the mid-second century from the Sethian tradition. It is a voice and perspective representing the missing half of a conversation between sectarian Christians when Christianity was still in its youth.

The *Gospel of Judas* does not represent an actual historical dialogue between Jesus and his disciples, or between Jesus and Judas for that matter. In this Irenaeus was right: it is "fictitious history." But as fictitious history, it is at one and the same time "fiction" and "non-fiction." For those of us who really want to know what early Christianity was like, the *Gospel of Judas* is of tremendous historical value because it is a fictionalization of a conversation that the Sethian Christians were having with the apostolic Christians in the mid-second century. Jesus represents the voice of the Gnostics, while the twelve disciples are the voice of the apostolic Christians. Much can be gained from listening to their dialogue.

Some Christians in the past, like Bishop Irenaeus, wished to shut out this dissenting voice because it did not support the kind of religiosity, the kind of Christianity, that was their "truth." But now that the *Gospel of Judas* has resurfaced in the twenty-first century, its voice can be silenced no longer. This book is written to liberate its voice and lend an ear to its "truth."

CHAPTER 2

A Gnostic Catechism

As I translated the *Gospel of Judas*, I realized quite soon the
sectarian nature of the Gospel and its affinity with a peculiar brand
of ancient Gnosticism known as Sethianism. What this means, as
we have seen, is that the *Gospel of Judas* was written by Christians
who identified themselves outside and even against the apostolic
Christianity of the second century CE. These peculiar Christians
were esoterically minded. For them, God was not something to be
intellectually comprehended by thinking about him. Rather, God is
something to be experienced, directly apprehended by the believer.
This form of "knowing" is what they called "gnosis." This gnosis is
not an intellectual knowledge, but knowledge by acquaintance – as
in "getting to know" someone through an interpersonal relationship. This relationship is what changes us, they thought. It
transforms us, they argued, and transfigures us. The God–Self
relationship – gnosis – was an experience of transcendence, moving
us from a state of separation, from the sinful mortal condition, to
an eternal spiritual body and life united with God.

Because of this Gnostic perspective, Sethians believed that
God had mysteries that could only be known through revelation
unmediated by the Church, mysteries not present in the Church's
simplistic creeds and petty bureaucracy or the bombastic pedagogy
of its leaders. So they formed lodges and seminaries separate from
the apostolic churches, where they would go to study, contemplate,
pray, and receive initiation into the mysteries of the Kingdom of

God. From this vantage point, they challenged the theology and ritual practices of conventional Christianity, criticizing the apostolic Christians for their theological naïveté and ritual ineptitude.

What is Gnosticism?

Scholars today are struggling to answer the very stubborn question of what Gnosticism is. We have realized, after examining the Gnostic literature recovered in the 1940s from Nag Hammadi, Egypt, that the rubric "Gnosticism" is a misnomer. It is a modern term that contemporary scholars have invented, rather than a word that describes a historical religion. Scholars constructed the modern understanding of Gnosticism to help describe those groups in the ancient world whom the leaders of the apostolic churches identified as deviant or heretical. We understood these "heretical" Christians as participants within a larger religiosity, an umbrella religion we called Gnosticism. Gnosticism came to represent for us a form of religion in the ancient world that had turned against Judaism and Christianity, a perversion of traditional morality and piety as well as theology. It was described by scholars in the twentieth century as a form of religiosity characterized by a negative view of the world and human existence, succumbing to cosmic nihilism and deeply yearning for everything spiritual.

But this romantic vision has been called into question. Analysis of the Nag Hammadi texts has shown us that there was no generic Gnostic religion. This does not mean, however, that there were no Gnostics! Even though there was no Church of Gnosticism, there were a number of Jews and Christians who were esoterically oriented and yearned for Gnosis. Some of them formed conventicles, lodges or seminary circles apart from the synagogue or church, while others attended synagogue or church while also being part of one of these secret societies. The communities they formed were not part of an umbrella Gnostic religion, but instead were sharply distinct from each other, especially in terms of social location, ritual performances, and even theological systems. In other words, the various Gnostic Christians wouldn't have understood themselves to be members of the same religious community even though there were features of their religiosity that they held in common.

So who were the Gnostics? Where did they come from? Bishop Irenaeus, living in the late second century, knew of at least two groups of Christians who called themselves the "Gnostics." He uses the term "Gnostics" with reference to a very early sectarian group the "Barbeloites" (named after the Mother aspect of the supreme God, Barbelo), which appears to be the same group as the "Sethians" (named after their biblical hero, Seth, son of Adam and Eve).[1] He also uses the term when describing a later Christian sectarian group, the Carpocratians (named after their founder, Carpocrates), whose leader in Rome during the late second century was a woman by the name of Marcellina.[2]

Since the Sethians appear to be the oldest known sectarians to use the word to describe themselves, the search for the elusive Gnostics best begins with Sethian literature. We are fortunate enough to possess a significant collection of literature written by Sethian Gnostics, discovered accidentally by an Egyptian peasant in 1945. He had been digging for fertilizer or *sabakh*, a nitrate-rich soil, near Nag Hammadi when his mattock struck a clay pot. The pot turned out to be a cache of fourth-century Coptic books. Much of the literature in these books is suppressed texts written by Christians like the Gnostics. Many of these texts are Sethian.

The World Created by Plato

What the Sethian literature from the Nag Hammadi collection reveals is that these Gnostics were both Jews and Christians who wished to combine the biblical tradition with Platonic philosophy, the "science" of the day. Platonic philosophy in this period conformed to Ptolemaic cosmology, which had been developing for centuries to replace the classical cosmos of ancient civilizations. The classical cosmos consisted of heaven, earth, and an underworld known as Hades or Sheol. By the early second century CE, this view was being eclipsed. Claudius Ptolemy is known to have given this cosmological revolution its systematic formulation. This geocentric vision of our universe survived until the Renaissance, when the modern Copernican cosmos was adopted. In the Ptolemaic system, the earth was understood to be the center of the universe, rather than the sun. The earth was surrounded by seven heavens which were envisioned as concentric rings, and each ring was associated with one of the seven planets or "stars": the moon, Mercury, Venus, the sun, Mars, Jupiter, and Saturn (see Figure 3).

The Platonic philosophers in this era did not think that this universe was absolute Reality. Instead, absolute Reality consisted of what they called the world of Forms or Ideas, like justice, beauty, or goodness. While we as human beings are embodied and live in this universe, we can learn the effects of the Forms, but we cannot have direct knowledge of them, except perhaps in momentary flashes of recollection. This includes God, "the Good," who consists of the totality of the Forms. We can have no more than momentary intuitions of Reality, the Platonists said, because our universe is only a shadow or reflection of the perfect world of Forms.

Figure 4. The Ptolemaic Universe

The goal of human life was to rehabilitate the soul or *psyche*, which had become corrupted and weak when it separated from the Good and descended through the planetary realms, literally falling from the sky into the human body. To reinvigorate the soul, the human being must live in accordance with the most important virtues, relying on reason to subdue the soul's desires and emotions. Once the *psyche* was rehabilitated and released from the body at the moment of death, it would be pure enough and strong enough to ascend through the seven planetary realms and reunite with the Good.

Plato thought the rational soul or *psyche* was immortal and pre-existent. He believed that the soul originally came from the heavenly world of Forms. During its pre-existence, while it resided in the upper world, the soul knew the Forms. It began to be weighed down by emotion and desire, however, and fell to the earth, where it was attached to a body. Once born in a body, the *psyche* existed in a state of forgetfulness. One of the reasons for the pious life is that it allows the soul rare opportunities to have brief flashes, sudden memories of the world of Forms.

Plato's understanding of cosmogony, how the world was created, was relatively simple. Plato describes the Good as the supreme and highest being. Below this is the creator god, the Demiurge or Craftsman, also known as Mind. The Demiurge is the one who creates this world out of disordered matter on the basis of a model he has in his mind, a model consisting of the ideal Forms above him. The Demiurge gives the universe its own soul, which the Platonists called the World-Soul or World-*Psyche*. So the cosmos is perceived by the Platonists to be a living organic being.

Because Plato understood the cosmos later to be an eternal living organism, Platonists believed that it was characterized by two movements which were understood to be simultaneous, inevitable and timeless. These movements are descent and ascent. Descent was understood by these Platonists to be the automatic creativity of the higher aspects of the cosmos generating the lower aspects. This generation was seen as a reflex action of the higher being forming a being immediately below himself. This creative process took place through an intellectual activity – contemplation. The higher being contemplated either himself (if he was all that existed) or the being just above him (if he was one of many that existed). This contemplation led to the downward generation of the next being or level of Reality. This downward procession is necessary and eternal. It is called "emanating" and the resulting being is called an "emanation."

Even though the generated being is a reflection of whatever is contemplated, it is not as perfect as the contemplated being. It is only a mirror image or a copy. In our world, we might use the office copy-machine as an example. If I make a copy of the original, is the copy exactly like the original? Or is it less perfect? If I make a copy of the copy and so on, how degraded can it become and still be a copy of that original? The problem with the process of emanation is that an exact duplicate cannot be made, only a reflection of the original. This results in a created world that is not a perfect re-creation of Reality. It is a shadow reflection.

Ascent, the second natural movement of the universe according to the Platonists, is upward, the movement of the soul as it passes up through all the stages of being to its final union with the Good. This upward movement is also connected to contemplation. As the soul raises its sights to contemplate higher orders of being, it raises itself up. It experiences progressive transformation until it finally can reunite with God after death.

Bible Stories about Yahweh's Angel

This Platonic worldview was simply regarded as the true state of affairs for most ancient people living in the Mediterranean. It only became a problem for Jews (and later for Christians) because it did not coincide with the biblical tradition (in much the same way that the biblical tradition does not coincide with modern scientific theories of evolution) – the Genesis story tells us that God or Yahweh created the world, not a lesser Demiurge (or the Big Bang). Since these same Jews had assimilated the Jewish God to Plato's transcendent, perfect God, these same Jews also wrestled with their observations about the world we live in. It was far from perfect. In fact it was full of suffering and misery. They wondered how a perfect

God could create this imperfect world. Instead of questioning or denying the accuracy of the Platonic worldview, some first-century Jews embraced it and chose to combine Plato's concept of the Demiurge with a new interpretation of the Genesis story.

How did these truly ingenious religious thinkers do this? They turned to the biblical stories about a special angel called the Angel of Yahweh. This angel is utterly unique because it possesses God's sacred and personal name, Yahweh, and functions as God's personal manifestation on earth. He appears to Hagar by a spring in the wilderness, saying to her, "I will greatly multiply your descendants ... Behold, you are with child, and shall bear a son." Hagar is stunned following the visitation. She calls out "the Name of Yahweh" who had spoken to her. She asks, "Have I really seen him and remained alive after seeing him?"[3] Although this passage does not explicitly identify the Angel of Yahweh with Yahweh, it is susceptible to that interpretation. Hagar is convinced she has seen God himself, a vision that traditionally results in death.[4]

Another biblical story where this identification is quite pronounced is the account of Moses and the burning bush. In this narrative, the Angel of Yahweh appears to Moses in the burning bush, but whose voice speaks from the bush? Not the Angel's, but God's own voice calls forth, "Moses, Moses!" Moses hides his face because "he was afraid to look at God."[5]

In these and other biblical stories, God and his Angel appear to be interchangeable – or at least that was the conclusion drawn by some Jews in the first century after conducting these types of careful readings of their sacred scriptures. This premise allowed these Jews to infer further that it was this Angel named Yahweh, not God himself, who had created the world. When the word "Yahweh" appears in the creation story, it was understood to be a reference to this Angel, not God. They supported this argument by pointing to passages that included plural references to God, like Genesis 1.26, "Let *us* make man in *our* image, after *our* likeness." Since God doesn't exhibit human characteristics, while angels do, they also supported their argument by citing biblical passages that describe God in anthropomorphic terms, such as when Adam and Eve "heard the sound of Yahweh God walking in the garden in the cool of day."[6] This couldn't be describing God, who doesn't have feet, let alone walk. It must refer to the Yahweh Angel, they said.

This is the way the creator of the world became God's Angel instead of God in the eyes of some first-century Jews. They didn't seem to believe that monotheism was threatened, however, because God was still the only being worthy of worship. The Angel, they argued, was God's personal manifestation anyway. This is how all their theological problems were solved – the Bible remained intact, the "scientific" explanation of the universe's origin was retained, and the miseries of the world were explained.

Oppositional Gods in Gnostic Theology

What is so paradoxical is that this reasoning could *only* have occurred among people who were taught to believe every word of the Bible and to cling to the faith that "God is one." Only these people would have been inclined to save the Genesis story of creation by reinterpreting it in this fashion, a reinterpretation that would ultimately lead to the bifurcation of God and Gnostic theological systems of oppositional gods.

We are not sure exactly when or how this speculation turned into "Gnosticism." Some scholars argue that Gnostic oppositional theology was entirely a Jewish development and some that it was entirely Christian. My study of the materials has led me to think that it is both. As long as the Yahweh Angel remained connected to

God and acted as his agent, the theological system was not yet Gnostic. But as time passed and speculation continued, these religious thinkers would put pressure on this understanding until it collapsed and a complete split between God and his Angel occurred. The creator Angel came to be perceived as either a revolutionary, warring against the supreme God, or hubristic, prideful and ignorant of the presence of the supreme God.

How did belief in this split between the supreme God and his Angel arise? The first factor was scriptural. Jews and Christians who were familiar with the scriptures knew that Yahweh is described in terms that aren't very flattering. He himself admits to being "jealous" in one of the Ten Commandments – "I the Lord your God am a jealous God" – making generations of children suffer for the wickedness and sins of their fathers.[7] Because of Yahweh's jealousy, he was also known as a god of anger, destroying entire communities of people who stirred up his wrath.[8] He himself says in Isaiah, "I make weal and create woe, I am Yahweh."[9] He also appears ignorant on occasion. In the Garden of Eden, didn't Yahweh have to call out to Adam and Eve and ask them "Where are you?" because he didn't know their whereabouts?[10] A literal reading of these types of scriptural references came to play an important role in Gnostic characterizations of the Demiurge as oppositional and even evil.

The second factor was an interpenetration of the Jewish story about the revolt of Lucifer and his angels with the developing story about the Yahweh creator Angel, who was jealous, angry, and ignorant. These religious thinkers began to toy with the idea that the Demiurge Angel, like Lucifer, might have been acting in rebellion against the supreme God. If he was jealous, angry, and ignorant, was he like Lucifer, who led a revolt and was thrown down from the high places? Not all Gnostic systems understood the

Demiurge to be demonic, but certainly some Gnostic systems did, including Sethianism in its earliest phase. All Gnostic systems, however, did impose some of the elements from the Lucifer mythology onto their narratives about the Demiurge, particularly Lucifer's opposition to God.

The third factor was a theoretical consequence of the overlap of Platonic and Jewish mythology. The Platonic God was completely transcendent, beyond the universe. Yahweh lived at the top of the universe, in the seventh heaven. Once God was split into the supreme God and the Yahweh Angel, the supreme God was elevated to a transcendent realm far beyond the seventh heaven, leaving the Yahweh Angel spatially abandoned and ignorant of anything beyond the seventh heaven of the cosmos. This separation and large spatial gap between God and his Angel left room for speculation about how the separation between the two occurred.

Ultimately, these three factors led to the creation of a Gnostic theology of oppositional gods. The hallmark of this theology centers on an ongoing and momentous war between the supreme God and an arrogant, ignorant Demiurge who claims, as the scripture says, "there is no god besides me."[11] He creates the heavens and the earth and everything in it out of ignorance, or in revolt when a voice above him reveals that he is not alone.

God's Original Sin and Fall

The large spatial gap between God and his Angel not only invited speculation about how they became separated. The Gnostics also wondered who lived in between. In their theoretical speculations, they began filling the gap between the transcendent supreme God and the Yahweh Demiurge with a multitude of divine emanations called Aeons. These emanations were aspects or characteristics of

God that make up his Totality, a concept known as God's Fullness or Pleroma. Essentially this means that the Godhead is not a Trinity, as many Christians believe today. Rather the Gnostic Godhead consisted of a number of Aeons, which were all the various aspects of God living as a collective: aspects like Life, Truth, Thought, and Intention.

The most important Aeon for the Gnostic story was the last emanation, the female emanation Sophia, God's Wisdom. She was well known to Jews and Christians from their scriptures, and they found her story appealing since she was an angelic being who lived with God but who descended into lower and lower realms, even to earth.

Sophia was known as an angelic being who was very exalted, dwelling in the clouds of heaven.[12] In the Jewish scriptures, she has her own throne in the clouds, she speaks out in God's court, and she is sent down to Israel to reveal God's wisdom to human beings. A beautiful hymn is preserved in the Wisdom of Ben Sirach telling her story of lofty living and earthly lodging:

Sophia will praise herself,
And will glory in the midst of her people.
In the assembly of the Most High
She will open her mouth,
And in the presence of his host she will glory,
"I came forth from the mouth of the Most High,
and covered the earth like a mist.
I dwelt in high places,
And my throne was in a pillar of cloud.
Alone I have made the circuit of the vault of heaven
And have walked in the depths of the abyss.
In the waves of the sea, in the whole earth,

And in every people and nation I have gotten a possession.

Among all these I sought a resting place.

I sought in whose territory I might lodge."[13]

Sophia is described as the Holy Spirit who "pervades and penetrates all things." She is called "a pure emanation of the Glory of the Almighty," a "breath of the Power of God," a "reflection of eternal light," an "immaculate mirror" of God's activity, and "an image of God's goodness."[14] She was brought forth by God before the creation of the world, and she herself helped to create the world and everything in it.[15] Sophia is "a tree of life to those who lay hold of her; fortunate are those who embrace her."[16] She holds life in her hands, reveals God's insights to human beings, and protects and strengthens generations of human beings beginning with Adam.[17] She is even known as God's spouse, "an initiate in the knowledge of God, and an associate in his works."[18]

Because she is known in scripture to descend from heaven into the world and interact with humans, in Gnostic systems this Aeon becomes the one who crosses boundaries. She leaves the Pleroma and initiates the process of creation in the lower realms. Her fall out of the Pleroma is the moment in the emanation process that "errors out," so to speak, just as the process of serial photocopying eventually results in a copy that is no longer readable. Her movement out of the Pleroma is perceived as a downward spiral or "fall" into denser and denser realms of being. Her leaking spirit eventually lodges in human bodies, vessels of imprisonment and redemption.

This means that "original sin" does not occur in the Garden of Eden as a fault of human beings. Rather the original sin occurred in the Pleroma prior to the creation of the world, and this error led to God rupturing and Sophia falling out. The Gnostics speculated about what sin God could possibly commit, what sin could inevitably lead to his rupture. Since God existed as a single being, there are only two activities he could be involved in – thinking about himself, or giving pleasure to himself. The Gnostics toyed with both these paradigms, and their stories are penetrated with both images. Their descriptions of the emanation process include contemplative activities like thinking and reflecting, as well as erotic activities like masturbation and procreative sex.

So original sin has nothing to do with disobedient humans, but exists from the beginning within God's very own nature. It is narcissism – pride, vanity, and curiosity about himself. A very good example of this thinking can be found in the Sethian *Apocryphon of John*. The beginning of the emanation process is narcissistic – God looks into a pool of water, admiring himself. However, what he sees is his "spirit," his female image. Because she embodies his own desire and vanity, he acts, either pulling back from her or pushing her away. When he does this, she emerges as the "first power" shining in God's light. Her name is Barbelo, who is the "womb of everything." She is called "Mother–Father," the "Holy Spirit," and the "Androgynous One." From her emanate other divine aspects of God.[19]

The expansion of the Sethian Godhead is quite complicated, and the Sethian literature preserves many variations on this process. But there are some features common to all versions of the myth (displayed in Fig. 4). First, the Pleroma consists of three major Aeons – the Father, the Mother, and the Son. Second, these Aeons are all androgynous. The Father is an invisible "Spirit," who sees his female image when he peers into the reflecting pool. The Mother is the "first man," "thrice-male," "Womb," and "Triple Androgynous Name." The Son is the "Self-Generated," "First-Born," and "Only-Begotten." Third, the Father, Mother, and Son

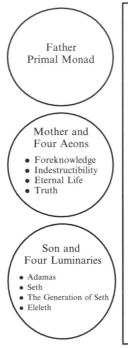

God as a Divine Triad

Invisible Spirit, Unknown Father, God and Father of Everything, Invisible, Unknowable, Incomprehensible, Ineffable, Nameless.

Barbelo (or: Barbero), Mother, Womb of Everything, Triple-Powered, First Power, First Thought, Forethought, Image of the Invisible Virginal Spirit, Glory, Mother–Father, First Man, Holy Spirit, Thrice-male, Triple-named. Barbelo is composed of four Aeons – Foreknowledge, Indestructibility, Eternal Life, and Truth. Together they make up the androgynous Pentad of Aeons, which is the Image of the Invisible Spirit. Because the Aeons are androgynous, containing both genders, Barbelo is also called the Decad of Aeons. In some later Platonized texts, Barbelo contains three Aeons: Kalyptos, Protophanes, and Autogenes.

Also called Autogenes, the Son is the only offspring of Barbelo and the Father. In some texts, Autogenes rests on a throne in the Aeon Domedon Doxomedon. With him are the angel Yoel, the Anointed; Esephekh, who is Autogenes' son; and Moirothea (or Plesithea), who is the mother of the four Luminaries.

Together these Aeons make up the Sethian Godhead, called the Pleroma or Fullness.

Figure 5. The Sethian Godhead

contain within themselves a number of other Aeons, as well as light-beings called Luminaries.

The *Gospel of Judas* narrates its version of the expansion of the Sethian Pleroma in a very abbreviated form. Jesus reveals that "there exists a great and boundless Aeon, whose extent no generation of angels has seen, [in] which is the great Invisible Spirit, that no eye of an angel has seen, no thought of the heart has comprehended, nor was it called by any name."[20] We also are told that "the immortal Aeon of Barbelo" exists.[21] As for the Son, Jesus tells us that he came into being when a cloud of light appeared and the Father said, "Let an angel come into being as my assistant."

The Son is born from the cloud, the "Self-Generated One, the God of Light."[22] Within the Son exist the standard Sethian realms of four Luminaries (Adamas, Seth, the Generation of Seth, and Eleleth) and a plethora of assistant angels, Aeons, and heavens.[23] The final Aeon to be generated within Eleleth is Sophia.[24]

The Gnostic Created Order

In the typical Sethian narrative of creation, it is Ialdabaoth who emerges as the prime creator god responsible for crafting our entire universe, from the top heaven to the spherical earth to the bottom abyss. The texts which relate the stories of his origin are quite ugly. His mother is Sophia and he is a monster because of the way Sophia generates him. Her androgyne splits, her female aspect wishing to create something without consulting her male aspect. So what she produces is imperfect: it isn't whole. The consequences of her desire take the form of a lion-faced serpent, with fire in his eyes. Sophia casts him away from herself, surrounds him with a luminous cloud to hide him, and names him Ialdabaoth.[25]

Ialdabaoth becomes strong and arrogant, and steals some of his mother's spirit before descending into lower regions. Residing in his cloud, his operations headquarters, he creates more assistants to help him rule over these lower regions. The names of his primary assistants who live with him in his cloud and work on his behalf are usually Saklas and Nebruel. These assistants are known as "Archons" or rulers. Ialdabaoth and his assistants create twelve more great Archons to rule the twelve realms below their cloud – the seven heavens and the five abysses. Each of these Archons in turn creates a number of lesser angels as assistants to populate their own realms.

In the *Gospel of Judas*, Ialdabaoth's identity is fused with

Nebruel, whom the author points out is also named "Apostate," meaning "Renegade" or "Traitor." He lives in the same cloud as Saklas. The two of them produce twelve Archons to populate the seven heavens and the five abysses. The *Gospel of Judas* only mentions the names of the five Archons who rule over the underworld – Atheth,[26] Harmathoth, Galila, Yobel, and Adonaios.[27] These Archons are the usual suspects who rule over the abysses in the Sethian myth.

After the Archons are produced, the typical Sethian narrative turns to the creation of the human being whose form is patterned after an image or likeness, either Ialdabaoth's own, or a reflection beamed down from above. This human being cannot stand, however, but writhes around on the ground like a worm. So Sophia whispers in Ialdabaoth's ear, secretly telling him to blow his breath into the nostrils of his creature. When he does this, he unknowingly disperses his share of his mother's stolen spirit within the human *psyche* or soul. Since Ialdabaoth has breathed out the Spirit, he no longer possesses it. Its dispersal within the human being will make it possible for Sophia to retrieve it. But this also means that Ialdabaoth can fight for it too. So the human being becomes the battleground of the gods.

The *Gospel of Judas* is very fragmentary at this point in its recounting of the Sethian story, but we hear that Saklas and his assistants were involved in the creation of Adam and Eve. Jesus and Judas engage in dialogue about the human spirit. According to this dialogue, Sophia is not the one who tricks Ialdabaoth to breathe the stolen spirit into the human's nostrils. Rather, the text just assumes that two types of spirit exist. These spirits are similar to the types mentioned in other Sethian literature. According to the *Apocryphon of John*, the Archons create a "counterfeit" spirit resembling Sophia's but which they use to pollute some of the human souls.[28] In the *Gospel of Judas*, the better of the two spirits (equivalent to Sophia's spirit) is guarded by Gabriel, and given by him only to Gnostic babies, the generation without a king. The lesser type of spirit (equivalent to the counterfeit spirit) is given by Michael to the rest of the human generations, whose king is Ialdabaoth. The human generations with the counterfeit spirit are completely under the influence of the stars and fate. They will perish along with their stars.[29]

Gnostic Liberation

So God is at fault, but through no fault of his own. The flaw that leads to his rupture is an essential part of his nature – his unavoidable reflection upon himself, his self-absorption, his curiosity about his own being. Since the "fall" happened because of God rather than because of human error, the traditional interpretation of the creation story made no sense. So that interpretation was reversed in highly subversive ways, at least in the Sethian narrative. It became a paradigm for the enfeeblement of the spirit as well as its liberation. It is a story of trickery and skirmishes between Sophia and Ialdabaoth, who both want to retrieve her spirit for themselves. Ialdabaoth works to keep human beings distracted and ignorant of the supreme God and their true nature so that the spirit will not know about the supreme God, nor be able to find its way home. Sophia works along with an Illuminator sent down from the Father to redeem the spirit and return it to the supreme God, to repair the rupture, to assist God in saving himself.

So when Eve listens to the snake, this is a good thing, a moment of redemption when her spirit is awakened from its slumber. In Christian Sethian texts, the snake sometimes is said to be Christ himself come down from the upper Aeon, granting Eve and Adam gnosis when they eat of the Tree. So the *Gospel of Judas* relates, "God caused gnosis to be [given] to Adam and those with him, so that the Archons of Chaos and Hades would not rule over them."[30]

In the typical Sethian story, this makes Ialdabaoth irate. So he casts Adam and Eve out of Paradise into yet lower realms of the world. This changes Adam and Eve's bodies to very coarse matter and further corrupts and enfeebles their souls. They forget completely about the supreme God. They learn about sex and become distracted, bearing children – a process that further distributes the spirit, making its retrieval by God exponentially more difficult. Cain and Abel die before they bear children. So this activity falls to Seth and Norea, who become the primal ancestors of all humankind. God intervenes in their lives in various ways. Seth and Norea receive instruction from the Illuminator about the supreme God, their true nature, and the presumptuousness of Ialdabaoth.

The Demiurge again is enraged and plans a flood to wipe them out. But before he can do this, Seth writes down on stone tablets, to preserve them from the flood, the secret rituals and liturgies God taught them to use, liturgies that would release their spirits and allow them to return to God. The Sethian Christians claimed that the tablets did survive the flood. They possessed a manuscript copy of this liturgy supposedly written by Seth, a beautiful threefold hymn collection called the *Three Steles of Seth*. A copy of this text is in the Nag Hammadi collection.

This war game between God and Ialdabaoth continued throughout human history. For every move God made to redeem the spirit (when God sent down an Aeon as an Illuminator) Ialdabaoth made a countermove to stop it. God's redemptive move always involved an awakening of the human spirit, instruction about the presence of the supreme God and how to get back to him. In the Sethian tradition, the way to get back to him involved a cluster of elaborate initiation rituals they called the "Five Seals." These rituals released the spirit so that it could practice ascending out of the cosmic realms, and journey into the Aeons of the Pleroma.

The Sethian Gnostics appear to have held these initiation ceremonies in their lodges or seminaries, using baptism, anointing, prayer, hymn-singing, intonation and contemplation to make these dangerous spirit journeys. At each level of ascent, these baptisms, anointings and intonations were repeated several times, with the result that the person would experience a gradual transformation of the spirit as it journeyed upward. Often we find in their texts the intonation of the seven vowels. The Greeks believed that these vowels corresponded to the sounds of the planets, each of which had its own tone. Pronounced together, they produced the harmony of the seven spheres. These harmonies were frequently pronounced by Egyptian priests in temples and were meant to charm the gods. The Sethians used other intonations in conjunction with these, including calling out the names of the Aeons to capture their power for the ascent. Ultimately, these practices were trial runs, progressively showing the spirit its way out of the cosmos, its way home. At death, when the spirit was liberated from the body, it was free to ascend through the cosmic girdle and into the upper Aeon, coming to rest in God's bosom.

Where does Jesus' death fit into this story? In Sethian Christianity, Jesus is the last Illuminator, who descends from the Father, provides instruction about the supreme God, and shares with his Gnostic followers the ceremony of the "Five Seals." His advent is God's best move in the war game, and his crucifixion is

Ialdabaoth's worst countermove. For when Ialdabaoth crucifies Jesus, his countermove is his final ploy. Much to his suprise, his move releases Jesus' powerful spirit from his body. Unlike other human spirits, Jesus' spirit cannot be detained by Ialdabaoth. It is different. It is an Aeon. Jesus' spirit shoots up through the cosmic atmosphere, carving out a path to the Upper Kingdom and conquering the Archons along the way. In this way, Jesus brings about the end of Ialdabaoth's control over the human spirit, and God saves himself.

PART 2

Translation Matters

CHAPTER 3

A Mistaken Gospel

The name alone gives us pause. The *Gospel of Judas*? What good news could Judas possibly possess? Wasn't he a traitor to Jesus, possessed by a demon, betraying him with a kiss? On April 9, 2006, National Geographic and a select team of scholars shocked the world when it released its interpretation and English translation of the *Gospel of Judas*, along with a full-length documentary and novella that sketched the intrigue of its mysterious discovery and underground recovery.[1]

Its discovery as an Egyptian antiquity is certain, but it is anyone's guess exactly who found it and where. In the year 2000, after being on the market for nearly twenty years, it was finally purchased by a Swiss antiquities dealer, Freida Nussberger-Tchacos, for $300,000. Even I, who had known for years about the manuscript languishing in a bank vault in Hicksville, New York, was glued to the tube, as I watched, with utter fascination, my colleagues report their discovery on the National Geographic Channel, and read headline after headline about the "good news" of the *Gospel of Judas*.

What we heard was that the "good news" is that Judas, in this Gospel, is not an evil man possessed by demon or Satan to betray Jesus as he is in the Gospels of Luke and John. Rather, we were told that Judas Iscariot is "the perfect Gnostic," a man so worthy that, by the end of his Gospel, he is "transfigured," ascending into a luminous cloud where he will receive a divine vision.[2]

We listened as the scholars involved reported that Judas is perfect because he has been "enlightened," exclusively learning at the feet of Jesus about the divine world and the divine light within him.[3] In his Gospel, Judas is the blessed one, not the cursed one. He is called the thirteenth "spirit" whose blessed star will ascend beyond the stars of the other disciples. Thirteen, in fact, is Judas' "lucky number."[4]

We were told that Judas' betrayal in his Gospel is not an evil act, but a "righteous act," one that earns him the right to "surpass" all the other disciples. "By handing Jesus over to the authorities," Professor Erhman said, "Judas allows Jesus to escape his own mortal flesh to return to his eternal home."[5]

We heard that when Jesus says to Judas in the Gospel, "But you will exceed all of them. For you will sacrifice the man that clothes me," Jesus is begging Judas to release his soul. The other disciples will offer other sacrifices, "but what Judas will do is the best gift of all," Professor Meyer stated. "Judas could do no less for his friend and soul mate, and he betrays him. That is the good news of the *Gospel of Judas*."[6]

With such a sensational release and intriguing interpretation, I wanted nothing better than to spend a few days in my office translating the old Coptic Gospel for myself. So I downloaded the Coptic transcription of the *Gospel of Judas* from the National Geographic website as soon as it was posted that April.[7] But I quickly became frustrated because National Geographic did not release photographs of the manuscript pages. So I could not check the accuracy of the transcription, or critically evaluate it, or offer alternative readings for troublesome areas in the manuscript. I had to trust what they had provided.

It wasn't long before I began to become concerned with their English translation of several passages of the Coptic, translations that appeared to me not only faulty, but faulty in a certain way. Their translation of several phrases supported their provocative and sensationalist interpretation, while my "corrected" translation did not. As I translated line after line, I became increasingly concerned, wondering what was going on, since my translation of the Gospel suggested that Judas was as evil as ever, and certainly no Gnostic.

I was (and still am) uneasy about this, because I consider several members of the team to be personal friends, as well as colleagues. The work that they have put into the restoration of this manuscript is not only commendable but incredible, taking bits and pieces – mere scraps in many cases – of papyri and piecing them together with the help of state-of-the-art computer technology.

The manuscript was in the worst shape possible, barely surviving its poor handling, including a stay in a freezer. One of its early owners thought that freezing the manuscript would keep the humidity from degrading the text. He failed to realize, however, that papyrus is paper made from plants whose cells hold water. So once the manuscript thawed – as you can well imagine – it fell to pieces. By the time the conservationists received it, much of it lay in thousands of fragments scattered like crumbs. Professor Kasser, Florence Darby, and Gregor Wurst used tweezers to put the fragmented pieces back together again. At least 15 per cent of the manuscript is lost forever, crumbled into particles as fine as sand.

So without their painstaking, exhaustive labor over several years, we would not have a manuscript to read at all, let alone a manuscript over which to disagree about matters of translation and interpretation. But there I sat, with the transcription in front of me, nonetheless quite perplexed about the translation choices Professors Kasser, Meyer, and Wurst had made.[8] Even though some of the choices appear to be minor – one word, a preposition, a letter –

they are not minutiae. They call into serious question the team's provocative interpretation of Judas as Jesus' beloved and confidant.

"Spirit" or "Demon"

What translation problems did I discover as I worked through the Coptic myself? One of the most egregious is found on p. 44 of the *Gospel of Judas*, where Jesus mocks Judas, addressing him by the name "Thirteenth Demon (*daimon*)."[9] In this case, the Greek loanword *daimon* (demon) occurs as a formal address to Judas. The National Geographic team translated this word "spirit."[10]

> *National Geographic Translation*
> And when Jesus heard this, he laughed and said to him, "You thirteenth *spirit*, why do you try so hard?"

> *Corrected Translation*
> When Jesus heard (this), he laughed. He said to him, "Why do you compete (with them), O Thirteenth *Demon*?"

"Spirit" is standardly chosen to translate the word *pneuma* when it occurs in a manuscript original. By the way, *pneuma* is used regularly throughout the *Gospel of Judas*, but not here![11] In a footnote, the National Geographic team makes an attempt to explain this odd translation, suggesting that it reflects Plato's use of the word in his famous work, the *Symposium*.[12]

The difficulty with this type of justification is that Plato's writings are almost five hundred years earlier than the *Gospel of Judas* and were written within a completely different conceptual environment. A lot happened to the word *daimon* in half a millennium. It is true that, in *pre-Christian* sources, the word *daimon* did have a broad meaning, and was used by Greek writers in the Hellenistic period to denote the concept of higher powers that lay beyond human capacity, whether for good or evil.[13] In some *pre-Christian* sources, it is even used to denote the "divine."[14] So in early popular Greek thought, the *daimon* is connected to concepts such as fate and destiny, as a higher power that overtakes a person and controls his fortune. For this reason, stars were called *daimones* (pl.), abstract forces or intermediary personal beings that controlled the cosmos and the fate of human beings.[15]

In much later Greek philosophical writings, however, *daimones* are associated with human emotions that corrupt our souls, wreaking havoc on any rational or reasonable thoughts we might wish to entertain. In these writings the *daimones* become more and more wicked. The philosophers demote them spatially in the cosmos, lowering their residences from stars to the air immediately surrounding the earth, as far away from God as possible.[16]

One can imagine what happens to the *daimones* in early Jewish and Christian literature, literature based on an understanding of our world in which Satan and his fallen angels hover in the atmosphere immediately surrounding the earth. The Jews and Christians conceived of the world in very different terms than we do today. The atmosphere around the earth was inhabited by the angels who had revolted against God at the beginning of time, angels that were led by Lucifer and cast down from the heights of heaven. These fallen angels continue their war against God in the lower atmosphere as a demonic host tempting, tormenting, and corrupting human souls. At the same time this demonic host is engaged in skirmishes against God's army of loyal angels led by Michael. At the end of time, there will be a final battle between these two armies, and God will finally triumph, binding Satan and his angels in a pit, and condemning the wicked of the earth to join them.

Given this cosmology, in early Jewish and Christian literature *daimones* are amalgamated with the demonic host and evil spirits that war against God and possess human beings, tempting them to wickedness.[17] In the New Testament and other early Christian literature, *daimones* are not divine spirits or intermediaries between human beings and God. In fact, they are antithetical to angels, radically distinct.[18] The *daimon* is a demon, in contrast to a benevolent spirit. The Christian literature in the early period (as well as the medieval period) contains hundreds of references to words built from the word *daimon*. In all cases, they refer to demons, evil spirits, and devils (*daimonon, daimonissa*), demon possession (*daimonao, daimoniakos, daimoniaris, daimoniasos, diamonidzomai, daimonioleptos, daimonismos, daimoniodos, daimoniodes*) and devilish behavior (*daimonodes*).[19]

The identification of the *daimon* with the supernatural host of evil spirits that populate the realms surrounding the earth is even more sinister in the Gnostic Christian literature, since the heavens are populated by rebellious Archons. One principal Archon rules each of the heavens, and each of them is identified with the planet or star that resides in that particular heaven. The Archons are exceedingly wicked, engaged in a war against the supreme God, who lives in a transcendent realm or Aeon far away. So the beings that live in the realms immediately surrounding the earth are Archons and their assistants. When the word *daimon* is used in Gnostic sources, it is applied frequently and consistently to the rebellious Archons and their malicious assistants.[20] For instance, in the *Holy Book of the Great Invisible Spirit*, the Archon Nebruel is called "a great *daimon*" with reference to his malicious power.[21] There is no doubt in my mind whatsoever that for a Gnostic

Christian text like the *Gospel of Judas*, to call Judas the "Thirteenth *Daimon*" is to identify him with a demon and an Archon, not a benevolent spirit as the National Geographic translation would have us believe.

"Set me apart for" or "separated me from"

The next problem that I noticed is on p. 46 of the *Gospel of Judas*, where the Coptic phrase "*pōrj e*" is used. Judas asks Jesus what is so great about the fact that he has received esoteric teaching from Jesus, "because you have separated me from (*pōrj e*) that generation."[22] The National Geographic team renders the clause very differently: "because you have set me apart for (*pōrj e*) that generation."[23]

National Geographic Translation
When Judas heard this, he said to him, "What is the advantage that I have received? For you have *set me apart for* that generation."

Corrected Translation
When Judas heard this, he said to him, "What is the advantage I received, since you have *separated me from* that generation?"

First of all, the National Geographic translation is nonsensical given its context. Why would Judas be upset about receiving esoteric teaching if he were to be included in the holy generation? Clearly he wouldn't.

Second and more important, it is grammatically impossible to translate the Coptic expression "*pōrj e*" in the way that the National Geographic team has done. The phrase in question consists of a

Coptic verb, *pōrj*, whose dictionary meaning is "to divide; be divided; or separate." Some verbs in Coptic form links with various prepositions that follow them. In these cases, the verb–preposition unit has its own dictionary meaning.[24] The preposition that follows *pōrj* is "*e.*" Together as a unit their dictionary meaning is "to be divided or separated from." In other words, these two words together have a fixed dictionary meaning, and that meaning is "to separate from," and never "to set apart for."[25]

The difference that this makes in our sentence is striking indeed. Judas has not been set apart to belong to the holy generation, as the National Geographic translation suggests. My corrected translation reads completely the opposite: Judas is upset because he has received esoteric teaching from Jesus, teaching which he sees as useless because he has been separated from the Gnostic generation who populate the upper world.

"Could it be that my seed is under the control of the rulers?" or "At no time may my seed control the archons!"

In a dream vision, Judas runs away from the twelve disciples and comes to a house. He sees prominent people in that house. He thinks that his dream means he will get to enter the Kingdom beyond this world. So he asks Jesus to allow him to enter the house. But Jesus tells Judas that he has been misled to think that he could possibly enter this realm, since it is reserved for the Gnostics and angels. The rest of humanity, including Judas, is under the rule of the stars. The text is incomplete but Jesus appears to accuse Judas of being the leader of the twelve Archons. Judas responds by crying out to Jesus, "Teacher, enough! At no time may my seed control the Archons!"[26] This is another passage in the Coptic that is problematic in the English translation given by National Geographic. The English rendering by the team has, "could it be that my seed is under the control of the rulers?"[27]

National Geographic Translation
Judas said, "Master, *could it be that my seed is under the control of the rulers?*"

Corrected Translation
Judas said, "Teacher, enough! *At no time may my seed control the Archons!*"

The Coptic here is not in the form of a question at all.[28] Judas is not asking Jesus a question. Rather he is making a very emphatic statement, an exclamation. This is indicated by the presence of the emphatic word "*ho*". The meaning of the Coptic would be better rendered by ending the sentence with an exclamation mark![29] A translation of this sentence should also reflect the sense of the original, "may it never be," lest something should happen that Judas doesn't want to happen.

So Judas is not questioning whether the Archons might be controlling him. Rather he is contradicting Jesus, exclaiming that he does not want to hear Jesus prophesy about his future demise when he becomes the Thirteenth Demon, Ialdabaoth, the King of the Archons. Furthermore, Jesus does not back down from his prediction. Rather he reaffirms this prophecy in the following sentences by telling Judas that, even though he will rule over the Archons, he will be overcome with lamentation.[30]

"Your ascent" or "You will not ascend"

The National Geographic team understands Judas' rule over the Archons to be an exaltation, an ascent beyond the cosmos into the upper Aeon. Judas the Gnostic is to be blessed with life eternal in the Kingdom of the supreme God. This interpretation is premised entirely on a faulty transcription and translation at the bottom of p. 46, where the last line is very fragmentary.[31] A terrible mistake has been made in their reconstruction of the Coptic. The way they have reconstructed the line is not only grammatically impossible in Coptic, but the portion of the manuscript where the Coptic is clear has been changed dramatically.

The change involves adding one letter, an *n*, to the front of the Coptic verb in the sentence. Without the *n* the main verb of the sentence is a negative future tense, indicating that Judas "will not ascend." The addition of the *n* on the front of the verb erases the negative from the sentence, so that the National Geographic translation erroneously reads that Judas *will* ascend. What this means is that the line in the Coptic manuscript without the National Geographic "emendation" says that Judas "will not ascend" to the holy generation!

National Geographic Translation
They will curse *your ascent* to the holy [generation].

Corrected Translation
And *you will not ascend* to the holy [generation].

There are further problems with this portion of the manuscript since the end of the preceding line, 24, does not appear to connect grammatically with the beginning of l. 24. In other words, there is no way to go from the end of l. 24 to the beginning of l. 25. It is not a sentence, but a sentence that is broken in midstream. The end of l. 24 is the pronoun "they" (*se*) as the subject of the sentence. Grammatically a verb must follow, and in this case it would be a future tense. So the sentence we would expect should read, "They will . . ." But that is not what we have. The manuscript instead reads "they" followed by "to you and" (*nak auo*) at the start of l. 25. What the National Geographic team did to remedy this problem is to read "to you and" (*nak auo*) as an abbreviation of a Greek loanword, *kataraomai*, "to curse," with a future-tense marker on the first word, "*na*" – thus they parsed the phrase *na-kauo*. The problem is that the abbreviation *kauo* never occurs in Greek or Coptic literature. *Kataraomai* never contracts to *kauo*.

I puzzled over the line for a few days and laid out how the lines might be reconstructed. If we relied only on what Coptic the manuscript actually has, we would have:

p. 1.

l. 46.24	They
l. 46.25	to you. And you will not ascend to
l. 47.1	the holy [generation].

What could this mean? I began to wonder if scribal error might not have come into play, if a line or two might not have dropped out between "They" and "to you" when the manuscript was being translated or copied by a scribe. If this were the case, then we would have:

l. 46.24	They
missing lines	[. . .]
l. 46.25	to you. And you will not ascend to

l. 47.1   the holy [generation].

Because I found the National Geographic team's reconstruction so puzzling, and because none but the team members have access to the manuscript or photographs of it, I contacted Marvin Meyer to discuss these lines of the manuscript. But he could not discuss the manuscript, having signed a non-disclosure statement in order to be part of the National Geographic team. A few weeks later, I flew to Paris and presented a paper on the *Gospel of Judas* at a conference devoted to that Gospel at the Sorbonne. In attendance were Marvin Meyer and Gregor Wurst, two of the team members responsible for the Coptic transcription and translation. They told those of us attending the conference that they have reconsidered this area of the manuscript since their initial publication of their book *The Gospel of Judas*. They had independently come to the same conclusion as I (and other scholars present) had. So in the critical edition of *The Gospel of Judas* just released, the lines in question are reconstructed, "they < will — > to you, and that you will not ascend on high to the holy [generation]."[32]

This corrected reconstruction is entirely opposite the first reconstruction published by the team, a reconstruction that served as the only evidence of Judas' ascent into the upper Aeon in the *Gospel of Judas*. What the Coptic manuscript actually does is deny Judas such an ascent. Unfortunately, the translation recently published by Professor Karen King in her book co-authored with Professor Elaine Pagels also follows this mistaken reconstruction, and it has influenced their commentary and understanding of Judas.[33] Also unfortunate are bold and completely wrong assessments about Judas' identity as a truly holy Gnostic already being published by scholars who have based their interpretations on the faulty reconstruction and English translation put out by

National Geographic. The following statement by Professor Bart Ehrman, for instance, adduces this very line as *the* support for his interpretation of Judas in his new book *The Lost Gospel of Judas Iscariot*: "Judas will transcend the Twelve, who continue to think the creator god of this world is the true God, and he will enter into the truth. Upon his death (when they stone him), he will ascend 'to the holy [generation]' (46.23–47.1)."[34] Without this fictitious Coptic line, there is no ascent of Judas into the holy generation.

"You will exceed all of them" or "You will do worse than all of them"

The English translation that most surprised me is of two lines on p. 56 of the *Gospel of Judas*.[35] The Coptic literally reads: "You will do more than all of them. For the man who clothes me, you will sacrifice him." The National Geographic team gives a different translation: "But you will exceed all of them. For you will sacrifice the man that clothes me."[36]

The translation "exceed" has a positive English connotation that does not accurately render the Coptic expression, "*er-houo eroou terou*," in its immediate context. The phrase consists of the verb "to be" (*er*), which is coupled with a noun, "the greater part" (*houo*), followed by a preposition, "*e*." Together these words make up the fixed expression "to be more than." Now the question is, "to be more than" what? The answer is always determined by the immediate context of the phrase.[37]

What is the context of this phrase on p. 56 of the *Gospel of Judas*? It is negative, although this is not readily noticeable in the National Geographic team's translation because the sentence in question has been separated from its negative context with the introduction of a new paragraph at this point.

National Geographic Translation
Truly [I] say to you, Judas, those [who] offer sacrifices to
Saklas < *several missing lines* > everything is evil.
But *you will exceed all of them.* For you will sacrifice the
man who bears me.

So the comparative expression "to be more than" has been
divorced from the discussion taking place between Jesus and
Judas by the creation of a new paragraph. Even so, it is clear that
the preceding discussion is negative. Jesus is talking to Judas
about the abhorrent behavior of those who sacrifice to the lower
god of the cosmos, Saklas, in a flashback to an earlier dream
vision of the twelve apostles, whom Jesus chastises for making
horrific sacrifices to the lower god. Jesus now says that all their
sacrifices are "evil."[38] He continues by telling Judas, "You will do
more than all of them. For the man which clothes me, you will
sacrifice him." The Coptic "do more than all of them" must mean
that Judas will do *more evil* than all the rest of the disciples, who
sacrifice lesser things to the Archons than Jesus himself. So the
best translation in English is:

Corrected Translation
Truly [I] say to you, Judas, those [who] offer sacrifices to
Saklas < *several missing lines* > everything that is evil. Yet *you*
will do worse than all of them. For the man that clothes me, you
will sacrifice him.

What Jesus is telling Judas is that Judas' sacrifice will be the worst
kind possible, because he will be sacrificing Jesus himself to the
Archons. Judas is not being asked by Jesus to release his soul from
the body, as Professor Bart Ehrman says; rather, the statement is a

prophecy from the lips of Jesus that Judas' action will result in another sacrifice to the Archons, and this action is an action worse than any of the rest of the disciples will ever commit.

"Your star has shone brightly" or "Your star has ascended"

On p. 56 of the *Gospel of Judas*, immediately following Jesus' prediction that Judas will offer the Archons the worst of all possible sacrifices (Jesus himself), Jesus quotes a series of psalms which are used as foreshadowing devices. The force of the quotations is to say to Judas that Jesus' prediction about Judas' involvement in his death is prophesied in the scriptures. One of the psalm lines has been translated by the National Geographic team, "Your star has shone brightly."[39]

> *National Geographic Translation*
> Your star has shone brightly.

I have not been able to determine how this translation was made, since it does not even come near to the dictionary definition of the Coptic verb *jōōbe*, which means "to pass by, over; to surpass, reach." It denotes ascendancy.[40] The intent of the phrase is not to reward Judas with a brightly shining star (as we were in grade school); rather it is to prophesy Judas' involvement in the death of Jesus. It is astrological lingo, indicating that Judas' star has ascended. This means that Judas is locked into this fate. He will bring about Jesus' death, and there is nothing he can do to stop his involvement in the affair.

Corrected Translation
Your star has ascended.

Several weeks into my translation project, the sensationalistic interpretation began to trouble me thoroughly. The translation choices made by the National Geographic team appeared to me to have led to the erroneous conclusion that Judas is a saint destined to join the holy generation of the Gnostics. The result is that certain claims have been made by National Geographic that the Gospel of Judas says certain things, things it just does *not* say:

- Judas is the perfect enlightened Gnostic.
- Judas ascends to the holy generation.
- Jesus wants Judas to betray him.
- Jesus wants to escape the material world.
- Judas performs a righteous act, serving Jesus by "betraying" him.
- Judas will be able to enter the divine realm as symbolized by his vision of the great house.
- As the "thirteenth," Judas surpasses the twelve disciples, and is lucky and blessed by this number.[41]

It appears to me that the National Geographic team's analysis has been further compromised because a number of the things that the *Gospel of Judas* really says have been either neglected or misunderstood:

- Judas is a demon.
- Judas will lament and mourn his fate.
- Judas' seed controls the Archons, instead of being controlled by them.

- Judas is separated from the holy generation.
- Judas will not ascend to the holy generation.
- Judas cannot enter the heavenly house he has seen in his vision.
- Judas does the worst thing he can do by sacrificing Jesus. [42]

The bottom line? The *Gospel of Judas* does not portray Judas as a hero or a Gnostic. What it does, however, is equally fascinating. It provides a mid-second-century Gnostic parody of Judas and his story, a parody that pokes fun at traditional Christian doctrines and practices. And Judas? Well, he is as evil as ever.

CHAPTER 4

The *Gospel of Judas* in English Translation

The *Gospel of Judas* is one manuscript within a larger papyrus codex or book. The book's modern designation is the Tchacos Codex, named after the Zurich antiquities dealer Frieda Nussberger-Tchacos, who bought the book after it had been on the market for twenty years. It made the long journey from the sands of Egypt to Europe to the United States, where it languished decaying in a bank vault. Frieda Tchacos says that she felt her own fate become entangled with the Codex and Judas in a terrible way, "like a curse."[1]

In 2001, she brought the Codex to Switzerland, met the famous Coptologist Professor Rudolphe Kasser, and set up a foundation to aid the restoration of the Codex. Eventually the National Geographic Society became involved and appointed a team of scholars to complete the restoration, translation, and interpretation of the Codex.

The Contents of the Tchacos Codex

Sixty-six pages have survived from this book. The *Gospel of Judas* is found on pp. 33 to 58. It is the only surviving copy from antiquity of the Gospel. The other documents within the book are a copy of the *Letter of Peter to Philip* (pp. 1–9), a text called *James* (pp. 10–22), and a fragment of the beginning of another work whose central figure is named Allogenes (pp. 59–66). The *Letter of Peter to Philip* is another copy of the text by the same name found in the Nag Hammadi collection. The version found in the Tchacos Codex is a fragmentary version of the fuller Coptic text preserved in Nag Hammadi Codex 8.

The second document's title, *James*, appears to be an abbreviation for its longer name, the *First Apocalypse of James*, which also survives in the Nag Hammadi collection, in Codex 5. The Nag Hammadi version of the apocalypse is fragmentary, so the *James* manuscript from the Tchacos Codex should help us recover a more complete reading of the *First Apocalypse of James*. There also appear to be significant variations in these two copies. This is not unusual in the world of scribal copying and preservation, but it will take some time for scholars to study the variations and establish a critical text of this apocalypse.

The title of the last text in the Tchacos Codex has not survived. Its contents do not match any known text that we possess. The beginning of the text is preserved, opening with a vision on Mount Tabor. The story features the figure Allogenes and also Satan. The story has some similarities with the temptation narratives in the New Testament Gospels, although it appears to be a Gnostic reuse of those narratives. It is unfortunate that this text is being called the *Book of Allogenes* when we have another completely different book by that name in the Nag Hammadi collection. I am sure that confusion will result. Perhaps we might differentiate it by calling it the *Book of Allogenes and Satan*?

The Qarara Books

The Tchacos Codex, however, is really only part of the story. It was not discovered alone. It was found in a limestone box with three other codices during an illegal excavation of a tomb near Jebel Qarara just north of Al Minya on the bank of the river Nile (see Fig. 1).[2] The other three books are known to us although they do not survive intact. They were divided into smaller portions by antiquities dealers who wished to profit financially from their sale. One of these books is a fourth- or fifth-century papyrus codex containing a Greek version of Exodus. The second is a fourth- or fifth-century papyrus book containing a Coptic translation of Paul's letters. The third is a portion of a mathematical treatise called the *Metrodological Tractate* and written in Greek.

The Exodus Codex survives in pieces, scattered all over the world, in private collections as well as the collections of the Ashland Theological Seminary, the Bienecke Library, and the Schøyen collection.[3] It appears to be a very important version of Exodus.[4] The whereabouts of the Coptic letters of Paul remains largely a mystery. Most of what we know about them comes from the brief report written in 1983 by Stephen Emmel, who had the opportunity to view the codices when they were being offered for sale.[5] The mathematical treatise is a geometry book containing numerous illustrations. The treatise was divided in two by the antiquities dealer Bruce Ferrini and sold to two separate buyers – Lloyd E. Cotsen, who has donated his portion to Princeton University, and an anonymous private collector.[6]

Why was the Tchacos Codex, an old book containing Gnostic texts, buried in a box with these three other books? This is an important question that has yet to be answered. It appears to me, however, that, if nothing else, their burial together points to their privileged place in the life of an early Christian living in ancient Egypt, a Christian who seems to have had esoteric leanings. This ancient person buried with these books had no difficulty during his or her lifetime studying canonical favorites like Paul and Exodus alongside the Gnostic *Gospel of Judas*. As for the mathematical treatise, its burial along with these others should not be that surprising given that both the Hermetics and Gnostics studied mathematical theorems in order to understand and map their universe.

Editorial Signs

In my translation of the *Gospel of Judas*, I use square brackets – [,] – to enclose fairly certain reconstructions of damaged areas of the manuscript, [. . .] to indicate holes or unreadable areas of the manuscript, parentheses – (,) – to enclose words that are not in the Coptic manuscript but are necessary to capture the meaning of the Coptic in English, angle brackets – <, > – to signal that an entire line is absent in the Coptic manuscript, and braces – {, } – to enclose letters and words that are mistakes in the Coptic uncorrected by the scribe. The subheadings are my own interpolations, meant to assist the reader through the unfamiliar narrative of this Gospel.

At this time, the critical edition of the Tchacos Codex has just been released by National Geographic. Now begins the long and arduous process of critically evaluating the transcription against the photographs and the originals. So any translation remains provisional until this evaluation is completed. Once the entire Codex is restored, it will be returned to Egypt to be permanently housed in the Coptic Museum in Old Cairo.

Page 33 of Codex Tchacos
Gospel of Judas

Opening Salutation

33.1   The secret revelatory discourse
33.2   in which Jesus spoke with Judas
33.3   Iscariot, for
33.4   eight days, three
33.5   days before he celebrated
33.6   Passover. When he appeared
33.7   on earth, he did
33.8   miracles and great signs
33.9   for the salvation of humanity.
33.10   And some [walked]
33.11   in the way of righteousness,
33.12   while others walked in their
33.13   sin. The twelve disciples
33.14   were called.
33.15   He started to speak with
33.16   them about the mysteries that
33.17   are beyond the universe and the things
33.18   that would happen from then on.
33.19   Often he did not appear to his
33.20   disciples, but when necessary[7],
33.21   you would find him in their midst.

Jesus Critical of the Eucharist Offered by the Twelve Disciples

33.22   And he appeared in Judaea
33.23   to his disciples one day.
33.24   He found them sitting,
33.25   gathered together, practicing
33.26   godliness. When he
33.27   [approached] his disciples

Page 34 of Codex Tchacos
Gospel of Judas

34.1   gathered and seated, offering thanks
34.2   over the bread, [he] laughed.
34.3   The disciples said to him,
34.4   "Teacher, why are you laughing at [our]
34.5   eucharist? We have done what
34.6   is right." He answered, saying
34.7   to them, "I am not laughing at you.
34.8   You do not do this
34.9   by your own will, but by this,
34.10 your god [will] be worshiped."

Jesus Critical of the Confession Made by the Twelve Disciples

34.11 They said, "Teacher,
34.12 [are] you [not] the son of our ·
34.13 god?" Jesus said to them,
34.14 "How do [you] know me?
34.15 Truly, [I] tell you,
34.16 no generation will
34.17 know me from the people who are among
34.18 you." When the disciples heard
34.19 this, [they]
34.20 began to get annoyed and
34.21 angry, and they cursed him in
34.22 their hearts. When Jesus
34.23 saw their ignorance, [he said]
34.24 to them, "Why this angry uproar?
34.25 Has your god within
34.26 you and [his ...]

Page 35 of Codex Tchacos
Gospel of Judas

35.1	vexed your souls?
35.2	Whoever has the strength among you
35.3	men, let him bring forward the
35.4	perfect person, and let him stand
35.5	in front of me!"
35.6	And they all said,
35.7	"We have the strength." But their spirits
35.8	were not able to get up the courage to stand before him,
35.9	except Judas
35.10	Iscariot. He was able
35.11	to stand before him,
35.12	yet he could not look him
35.13	in the eyes. But he turned
35.14	away his face. Judas [said] to him,
35.15	"I know
35.16	who you are and from what place you have come.
35.17	You came from the immortal
35.18	Aeon of Barbelo,
35.19	and the one who sent you
35.20	is he whose name I am not worthy to speak."
35.21	Then Jesus, knowing
35.22	that he was thinking about something
35.23	exalted, said to him,
35.24	"Separate from them. I shall tell you
35.25	the mysteries of the Kingdom,
35.26	not so that you will go there,
35.27	but so that you will grieve greatly.

Page 36 of Codex Tchacos
Gospel of Judas

36.1	For someone else will take
36.2	your place so that the twelve
36.3	[disciples] will still
36.4	be complete before their god."
36.5	And Judas said to him,
36.6	"When will you tell me these things?
36.7	And (when) will the great
36.8	day of light dawn for the generation
36.9	[...]?" But after he
36.10	said these things, Jesus left him.

Jesus Critical of the Holiness of the Twelve Disciples

36.11	The next morning, after this happened,
36.12	he [appeared] to his disciples.
36.13	And they said to him, "Teacher,
36.14	where did you go? What did you do
36.15	when you left us?" Jesus said to them,
36.16	"I went to another great
36.17	holy generation."
36.18	His disciples said to him,
36.19	"Lord, who is the great generation
36.20	more exalted and holier than us,
36.21	(a generation) not in these realms?"
36.22	And after Jesus heard this,
36.23	he laughed. He said to them,
36.24	"Why are you wondering
36.25	in your heart about the
36.26	strong and holy generation?

Page 37 of Codex Tchacos
Gospel of Judas

37.1	Truly, [I] say to you,
37.2	whoever is born of this realm
37.3	will not see that generation.
37.4	Nor will an army of
37.5	angels of the stars rule
37.6	over that generation. Nor will
37.7	people of mortal birth be able to
37.8	associate with it, because that generation
37.9	does not come from [...]
37.10	who lives [...].
37.11	[The] generation of people among [you]
37.12	is from the human generation.
37.13	[...]
37.14	power that [...]
37.15	power [...]
37.16	[by] which you rule."
37.17	When [his] disciples heard this,
37.18	they were troubled in [their]
37.19	spirits, each one (of them). They could not
37.20	say a thing.

The Twelve Disciples Tell Jesus about their Nightmare

37.20	Jesus came to [them]
37.21	another day. They said to [him],
37.22	"Teacher, we saw you in a [vision],
37.23	for we saw great [dreams]
37.24	[this] night that has passed."
37.25	[He said], "Why have [you]
37.26	[...] have gone into hiding?"

Page 38 of Codex Tchacos
Gospel of Judas

38.1	Then they [said, "We saw]
38.2	a great [temple with a large] altar
38.3	[in it and] twelve
38.4	men - we say·
38.5	that they are priests. And a name

<missing line>

38.6	There was a crowd of people waiting
38.7	at that altar
38.8	{at the altar}
38.9	[until] the priests [finished]
38.10	[making] the offerings. [But] we
38.11	waited."
38.12	Jesus said, "What are
38.13	[the priests] like?" They
38.14	[said, "Some] were
38.15	[...] [for] two weeks.
38.16	[Others] were sacrificing
38.17	their own children.
38.18	Others (were sacrificing) their wives as a gift,
38.19	[and] they were humiliating each other.
38.20	Some were sleeping with men.
38.21	Some were [committing murder].
38.22	Yet others were committing a
38.23	number of sins and lawless acts.
38.24	And the men standing
38.25	[beside] the altar [were]
38.26	calling upon your [Name].

Page 39 of Codex Tchacos
Gospel of Judas

39.1	And while taking part in all
39.2	their murderous deeds, the sacrifices burned
39.3	there."
39.4	And after they had said this, [they] were
39.5	quiet because they were troubled.

Jesus Interprets the Disciples' Nightmare

39.6	Jesus said to them, "Why are you
39.7	troubled? Truly, I say
39.8	to you, all the priests
39.9	who were standing beside
39.10	that altar were calling
39.11	upon my Name. And also I say
39.12	to you, my Name has been written
39.13	upon this [...] of the generations
39.14	of the stars by the human generations,
39.15	[and] they have planted
39.16	in my Name fruitless trees
39.17	shamefully."
39.18	Jesus said to them, "You
39.19	are those you saw who presented the offerings
39.20	upon the altar. That one
39.21	is the god you worship,
39.22	and the twelve men
39.23	you saw are you.
39.24	And the animals that were
39.25	brought for sacrifice
39.26	are those you saw, who
39.27	are the crowd of people that you lead astray.

Page 40 of Codex Tchacos
Gospel of Judas

40.1   Beside that altar,
40.2   [...] will stand
40.3   and
40.4   in this way he will make use
40.5   of my Name. And generations
40.6   of the impious will remain faithful to him.
40.7   After him,
40.8   another man will stand up for
40.9   the [fornicators]. And another man
40.10   [will] stand up for the murderers of
40.11   [children]. Yet another man, (for) those who
40.12   sleep with men, and those who
40.13   fast, and the rest of
40.14   corruptions, lawless acts, and error,
40.15   and those who say,
40.16   'We are equal to the angels.'
40.17   And they are the stars that accomplish
40.18   everything. For it has been said,
40.19   to the human generations, 'Behold,
40.20   God has received
40.21   your sacrifice from the hands of
40.22   priests' - this one is the 'Deacon
40.23   of Error.' For the Lord who
40.24   commands this is the one who is Lord
40.25   over the universe. On the last
40.26   day, they will be guilty."

Page 41 of Codex Tchacos
Gospel of Judas

Jesus Instructs the Disciples and Judas

41.1	Jesus said [to them], "Stop
41.2	[sacrificing] [...]
41.3	which you [...]
41.4	over the altar, since they are over
41.5	your stars and your angels,
41.6	having already been brought to an end.
41.7	Let them be [...]
41.8	before you, and let them go
41.9	[...]
41.10	[...]
41.11	[...]
41.12	[...]
41.13	[...]
41.14	[...]
41.15	[...]
41.16	[...]
41.17	[...]
41.18	[...]
41.19	[...]
41.20	[...]
41.21	[...]
41.22	[...]
41.23	[...]
41.24	[...] generations
41.25	[...]. A baker cannot
41.26	feed all creation

Page 42 of Codex Tchacos

Gospel of Judas

42.1	under [heaven]. And
42.2	[...] to them
42.3	[...] and
42.4	[...] to us and
42.5	[...] Jesus said to them,
42.6	"Stop struggling
42.7	with me. Each one
42.8	of you has his own star,
42.9	[and every] one [...].
42.10	[...]
42.11	[...]
42.12	[...]
42.13	[...]
42.14	[...]
42.15	[...]
42.16	[...]
42.17	[...]
42.18	[...]
42.19	[...]
42.20	[...]
42.21	[...]
42.22	[...]
42.23	[...]
42.24	[...]
42.25	[...]
42.26	[...]

Page 43 of Codex Tchacos

Gospel of Judas

43.1	[...] he
43.2	came to those who [...] [from the spring] of the
43.3	tree of [...]
43.4	[the time] of this age [...]
43.5	for a while [...]
43.6	but he came to water God's Paradise
43.7	and the enduring [generation],
43.8	because [he] will
43.9	not corrupt the [watering of] that
43.10	generation but [...]
43.11	for all eternity."[8]
43.12	Judas said to [him, "Rabbi],
43.13	what type of fruit does
43.14	this generation have?" Jesus said,
43.15	"The souls of every human generation
43.16	will die. But when these
43.17	people have completed
43.18	the time of the kingdom
43.19	and the spirit leaves
43.20	them, then their bodies
43.21	will die. Their souls
43.22	will be enlivened and they will be taken
43.23	up." Judas said,
43.24	"What will the rest
43.25	of the human generations do?" Jesus said,
43.26	"It is not possible

Page 44 of Codex Tchacos
Gospel of Judas

44.1	to sow upon [rock] and get
44.2	fruit. In the same way,
44.3	[...] the [corrupted] generation
44.4	and the perishable Sophia
44.5	[...] the hand that created
44.6	mortal people, so that their souls
44.7	ascend to the eternal realms above.
44.8	Truly, I say to you,
44.9	[...] angel
44.10	[...] power can see
44.11	those [...]
44.12	[...] holy generation
44.13	[...]." After
44.14	Jesus said this, he left.

Judas Tells Jesus about his Dream

44.15	Judas said, "Teacher,
44.16	just as you have listened to all of them,
44.17	listen now also to me. For I have seen
44.18	a great vision." When Jesus
44.19	heard (this), he laughed.
44.20	He said to him, "Why do you compete
44.21	(with them), O Thirteenth Demon?
44.22	But speak up for yourself. I shall bear
44.23	with you." Judas said to him,
44.24	"I saw myself in the vision,
44.25	as the twelve
44.26	disciples threw stones at me,

Page 45 of Codex Tchacos
Gospel of Judas

45.1	chasing [me] [...]. And I also came
45.2	to the place [...] you.
45.3	I saw [a house] [...], and
45.4	its size my eyes could not [measure].
45.5	Important people were surrounding
45.6	it, and that house had a grass roof.
45.7	And
45.8	in the middle of the house was [a]
45.9	[crowd] [...]
45.10	[...]
45.11	Teacher, take me inside (the house) with
45.12	these people!"

Jesus Interprets Judas' Dream

45.12	[Jesus] answered him,
45.13	"Your star has led you astray,
45.14	O Judas," and
45.15	"No one born of any mortal is worthy
45.16	to enter
45.17	the house which you saw, because
45.18	that place is
45.19	reserved for the saints.
45.20	There neither the sun nor the moon
45.21	will rule, nor the day.
45.22	But (the saints) will stand there
45.23	forever, in the Aeon with
45.24	the holy angels. Behold,
45.25	I have told you the
45.26	mysteries of the Kingdom

Page 46 of Codex Tchacos
Gospel of Judas

46.1	and I have taught you about [the] error
46.2	of the stars. And [...] sent
46.3	[...] over
46.4	the twelve realms."

Judas and Jesus Disagree about the Meaning of Judas' Dream

46.5	Judas said, "Teacher,
46.6	enough! At no time may my seed control[9]
46.7	the Archons!" Jesus answered,
46.8	saying to him, "Come, let me
46.9	[tell] you that [...]
46.10	[...]
46.11	[...] but that you will
46.12	grieve much more, seeing
46.13	the Kingdom and all its generation."
46.14	When Judas heard
46.15	this, he said
46.16	to him, "What is the advantage
46.17	I received, since you have separated me from that
46.18	generation?" Jesus answered,
46.19	saying, "You will become
46.20	the Thirteenth, and
46.21	you will be cursed by
46.22	the other generations and
46.23	will rule over
46.24	them. And in the last days, they
<missing lines>	
46.25	to you. And you will not ascend to

Page 47 of Codex Tchacos
Gospel of Judas

47.1   the holy [generation]."

Jesus Instructs Judas about the Sethian World

47.1   Jesus said,
47.2   "[Come], I will teach you
47.3   about the [secrets that]
47.4   [no] human [has]
47.5   seen. For there exists a great
47.6   and boundless Aeon, whose
47.7   extent no generation of angels
47.8   has seen, [in] which is the great
47.9   Invisible [Spirit],
47.10   that no eye of an [angel]
47.11   has seen, no thought
47.12   of the heart has comprehended, nor was it called
47.13   by any name.
47.14   And a luminous cloud appeared
47.15   there.
47.16   And he said, 'Let
47.17   an angel come into being as my
47.18   assistant.' And a great angel emerged from
47.19   the cloud,
47.20   the Self-Generated One, the God
47.21   of Light. And through him,
47.22   four other angels came into being
47.23   from another
47.24   cloud. And they came into being as the
47.25   assistants of the angel, Self-Generated.
47.26   And the Self-Generated One said,

Page 48 of Codex Tchacos

Gospel of Judas

48.1	'Let
48.2	[...] come into being.' And it came
48.3	into being [...]. And
48.4	he [created] the first Luminary
48.5	to rule over it. And
48.6	he said, 'Let angels come into being
48.7	to worship
48.8	him.' And there came into being
48.9	myriads without number. And he said,
48.10	'Let a Luminous Aeon come into being.'
48.11	And it came into being.
48.12	He created the second
48.13	Luminary to rule over it,
48.14	along with myriads of angels without
48.15	number for their worship. And in this way,
48.16	he created the rest
48.17	of the Luminary Aeons, and he
48.18	made them rule over them. And
48.19	he created them – myriads of
48.20	angels without number as their
48.21	helpers. And Adamas was
48.22	in the first cloud
48.23	of light that no
48.24	angel has seen
48.25	among all those called
48.26	'god.' And he

Page 49 of Codex Tchacos

Gospel of Judas

49.1   and [...]
49.2   there [...]
49.3   the image [...]
49.4   and after the likeness of [these]
49.5   angels. He revealed the
49.6   Incorruptible Generation of Seth [...]
49.7   the twelve [Aeons and]
49.8   the twenty-four [Luminaries].
49.9   He revealed seventy-two
49.10   Luminaries in the Incorruptible Generation,
49.11   in accordance with the will of the
49.12   Spirit. The seventy-two
49.13   Luminaries revealed on their own
49.14   three hundred and sixty Luminaries in the
49.15   Incorruptible Generation according to the
49.16   will of the Spirit so that
49.17   their number is five for each.
49.18   And their Father consists of the
49.19   twelve Aeons and twelve
49.20   Luminaries. And
49.21   for each Aeon, (there are) six
49.22   heavens so that there are
49.23   seventy-two heavens
49.24   for the seventy-two Luminaries,
49.25   and for each one

Page 50 of Codex Tchacos
Gospel of Judas

50.1	[of them (there are) five] firmaments,
50.2	[so that there are] three hundred and sixty
50.3	[firmaments in all. They] were given
50.4	authority and a great
50.5	army of angels
50.6	[without number] for glory and worship,
50.7	and [also] virgin
50.8	spirits, for glory and
50.9	[worship] of all the Aeons and
50.10	their heavens and their firmaments.
50.11	The multitude of those immortals
50.12	is called
50.13	'Cosmos,' that is
50.14	'Destruction,' by the Father
50.15	and his seventy-two Luminaries
50.16	who are with the Self-
50.17	Generated One and his seventy-two
50.18	Aeons. In that place,
50.19	the first human appeared
50.20	with his
50.21	incorruptible Powers.
50.22	In the Aeon that appeared
50.23	with his generation is
50.24	the cloud of knowledge
50.25	and the angel
50.26	who is called

Page 51 of Codex Tchacos
Gospel of Judas

51.1   El[eleth] [...]10
51.2   with [...]
51.3   Aeon [...]
51.4   After these things, [...] said,
51.5   'Let twelve angels come into being,
51.6   [to] rule
51.7   over Chaos and [Hades.]'
51.8   And behold,
51.9   from a cloud, an [angel] appeared,
51.10   whose face flashed with fire.
51.11   His appearance was corrupted with blood.
51.12   His name was Nebro(el),
51.13   which means,
51.14   'Apostate.'
51.15   Other people (call him) 'Ialdabaoth.'
51.16   Another angel also came from
51.17   the cloud, 'Saklas.' So Nebro(el)
51.18   created six angels -
51.19   also Saklas - to be assistants,
51.20   and these generated twelve
51.21   angels in the heavens
51.22   and they received their portions, each one
51.23   (of the angels) in the heavens.
51.24   The twelve Archons said
51.25   to the twelve angels,
51.26   'Let each one of you

Page 52 of Codex Tchacos
Gospel of Judas

52.1	[...] and let
52.2	[...] generation
52.3	[...]¹¹
52.4	[five] angels. The first
52.5	[is Ath]eth, the one who is called
52.6	the 'Good One.' The
52.7	second is Harmathoth, who is
52.8	[the evil eye].¹² The
52.9	[third] is Galila. The
52.10	fourth is Yobel. The
52.11	fifth is Adonaios. These
52.12	are the five who ruled over
52.13	Hades, and the first over
52.14	Chaos. Then Saklas said
52.15	to his angels,
52.16	'Let us create a human being according to
52.17	the likeness and according to the image.'
52.18	Then they fashioned Adam
52.19	and his wife Eve, who
52.20	is called in the cloud,
52.21	'Zoe.' For by this
52.22	name, all the generations seek
52.23	him, and each one
52.24	of them calls her
52.25	these names. Now Saklas did not

Page 53 of Codex Tchacos

Gospel of Judas

53.1	[command …]
53.2	except […]
53.3	the generations […]
53.4	this […]
53.5	And the [Archon] said to him,
53.6	'Your life will be […]
53.7	time with your children.' "
53.8	Then Judas said to Jesus, "[What]
53.9	is the longest that a person will live?"
53.10	Jesus said,
53.11	"Why are you surprised that Adam
53.12	and his generation received his
53.13	numbered days in the place
53.14	where he received his reign
53.15	of numbered (days) along with his
53.16	Archon?" Judas said to Jesus,

Jesus Answers Judas' Questions about the Fate of Human Beings

53.17	"Does the human spirit die?"
53.18	Jesus said, "This is the way.
53.19	God commanded
53.20	Michael to give spirits to
53.21	humans - on loan while they serve.
53.22	The Great One commanded
53.23	Gabriel to give spirits
53.24	to the great generation with no king -
53.25	the spirit along with the soul. Because
53.26	the [rest] of the souls

Page 54 of Codex Tchacos
Gospel of Judas

54.1	[…]
54.2	[…] light
54.3	[…]
54.4	[…] around
54.5	[…] your inner spirit
54.6	[which] you made to dwell in this
54.7	[flesh], from the generations of
54.8	angels. But God caused
54.9	knowledge to be [given] to Adam along with
54.10	those with him, so that the Kings
54.11	of Chaos and Hades
54.12	might not rule over them."
54.13	Judas said to Jesus,
54.14	"What will those generations do?"
54.15	Jesus said,
54.16	"Truly, I say to you,
54.17	the stars bring to an end
54.18	all of them. When
54.19	Saklas finishes the time
54.20	allotted to him,
54.21	their first star will come
54.22	with the generations.
54.23	And it will be accomplished,
54.24	what has been said. Then they will
54.25	fornicate in my Name and
54.26	kill their children

Page 55 of Codex Tchacos

Gospel of Judas

55.1	and will [...]
55.2	and will [...]
55.3	[...]
55.4	[...]
55.5	[...]
55.6	[...]
55.7	[...]
55.8	[...]
55.9	[...] [in] my Name.
55.10	And your star will [rule]
55.11	over the thirteenth Aeon."
55.12	Afterwards, Jesus laughed.
55.13	[Judas said,] "Teacher,
55.14	[why are you laughing at me?"]
55.15	[Jesus] answered, [saying,] "I am
55.16	not laughing [at you], but at the
55.17	error of the stars, that these six
55.18	stars wander with these five
55.19	warriors, and they all
55.20	will perish along with their creations."
55.21	Then Judas said to Jesus, "So
55.22	what will those do who have been baptized
55.23	in your Name?"
55.24	Jesus said, "Truly, I
55.25	say [to you], this baptism

Page 56 of Codex Tchacos

Gospel of Judas

56.1	[...] [in] my Name
56.2	[...]
56.3	[...]
56.4	[...]
56.5	[...]
56.6	[...]
56.7	[...]
56.8	[...]
56.9	[...]
56.10	[...] to me.

Jesus Predicts Judas' Fate

56.11	Truly, I say to you,
56.12	Judas, [those who] offer sacrifices to
56.13	Saklas [...] God [...]
56.14	[...]
56.15	[...]
56.16	[...]
56.17	everything that is evil. Yet you
56.18	will do worse than all of them.
56.19	For the man that clothes
56.20	me, you will sacrifice
56.21	him. Already your horn has been raised,
56.22	and your wrath kindled,
56.23	and your star ascended,
56.24	and your heart has [...].

Page 57 of Codex Tchacos

Gospel of Judas

57.1	Truly, [I say to you,] your
57.2	last [. . .]
57.3	[. . .] become
57.4	[. . .]
57.5	[. . .]
57.6	[. . .] grieve
57.7	[. . .]
57.8	[. . .] the
57.9	Archon who is destroyed. And then
57.10	the model
57.11	of the great generation of Adam will be exalted because
57.12	prior to heaven and earth and
57.13	angels, there exists that generation
57.14	from the Aeons.
57.15	Behold, you have been told everything.
57.16	Lift up your eyes and see the cloud
57.17	and the light in it,
57.18	and the stars around it.
57.19	The star which is leading
57.20	is your star."
57.21	Judas lifted his eyes.
57.22	He saw the luminous cloud and
57.23	he entered it. Those people
57.24	standing on the ground
57.25	heard a voice coming from
57.26	the cloud saying,

Page 58 of Codex Tchacos
Gospel of Judas

58.1   "[...] great
58.2   generation [...] image
58.3   [...]
58.4   [...]
58.5   [...]
58.6   [...]
58.7   [...]
58.8   [...]

Judas Betrays Jesus

58.9   [...] [Then] their high priests murmured
58.10   because [he]
58.11   had gone into the guest room for
58.12   his prayer. Some scribes were
58.13   there
58.14   watching carefully in order to
58.15   arrest him during the
58.16   prayer. For they were afraid
58.17   of the people, since he was
58.18   held by all as a prophet.
58.19   And they approached
58.20   Judas. They said to him,
58.21   "What are you doing here?
58.22   Aren't you the disciple of Jesus?"
58.23   He answered them
58.24   as they wished. Then Judas
58.25   received some money. He handed
58.26   him over to them.
58.27
58.28   The Gospel
58.29   of Judas

PART 3

Good Old Judas?

CHAPTER 5

Judas the Confessor

The *Gospel of Judas* opens during the week of Christ's passion, three days before the celebration of Passover. The Gospel begins with a brief salutation and overview of Jesus' life, stating that Jesus "appeared on earth" and performed "miracles and great signs for the salvation of humanity." Some people he met were righteous, and others were sinners. He called the twelve disciples and taught them about "the mysteries that are beyond the universe" as well as "the things that would happen from then on."[1]

In striking contrast to other Gospel stories, the author of the *Gospel of Judas* tells us that Jesus did not spend much time physically present among his disciples. He would only appear among them when absolutely "necessary."[2] Why? We are seeing here a Gnostic view of Jesus, that he spent most of his time ascended, in the upper Aeon, in the Kingdom of the saints and holy angels, beyond this universe with its lesser kingdoms or realms. Jesus is from the upper Aeon and belongs to it, only descending for revelatory purposes as he works to redeem humanity.

Jesus Critical of the Confession of the Twelve Apostles

One of Jesus' descents occurred in Judaea. Jesus finds his disciples sitting together in a cultic setting. They are praying, blessing a loaf of bread with eucharistic words. Jesus laughs at their performance, telling them that they are not worshiping the supreme God with these actions, but the lesser Demiurge. The room erupts with cries of outrage, and together the disciples confess Jesus as the "Son of our God."[3]

Their mutual confession is a remarkable midrash on the story commonly known as Peter's confession, first spun by the Markan author. In the traditional Markan story, Peter recognizes Jesus as "the Messiah":

> Jesus went on with his disciples, to the villages of Caesarea Philippi, and on the way he asked his disciples, "Who do people say that I am?" And they told him, "John the Baptist. And others say, Elijah. And others, one of the prophets." And he asked them, "But who do you say that I am?" Peter answered him, "You are the Messiah."[4]

In the Gospels of Matthew and Luke, the turn of phrase is different. Jesus is recognized by Peter as "the Messiah, the Son of the living God" in Matthew,[5] and "The Messiah of God" in Luke.[6]

Another version of the story came to light when the *Gospel of Thomas* was discovered as part of the Nag Hammadi collection. In this version, the disciple Thomas confesses Jesus' true identity:

> Jesus said to his disciples, "Speculate about me. Tell me, who am I like?" Simon Peter said to him, "You are like a righteous angel." Matthew said to him, "You are like a sage, a temperate person." Thomas said to him, "Master, my mouth cannot attempt to say whom you are like." Jesus said, "I am not your master. After you drank, you became intoxicated from the bubbling font which I had measured out." And he took him and retreated. He told him three words. Then when Thomas returned to his friends, they asked him, "What did Jesus say to you?" Thomas said to them,

"If I tell you one of the words which he told me, you will pick up stones and throw them at me. Then fire will come out of the stones and burn you up."[7]

Thomas' confession is quite remarkable in that it overrides two of the confessions of the other disciples (Peter and Matthew), who understand Jesus in terms of angels and sages. Since stoning is the punishment for blasphemy in early Judaism, it is quite certain that the secret words Jesus confided to Thomas included the pronunciation of the unutterable divine Name of God, Yahweh. So Thomas' confession places Jesus on the level of God, bearer of his great Name. This is quite consistent with the opinion of the author of the Gospel of John. In chap. 10, at the Feast of Dedication, Jesus declares, "I and the Father are one." Immediately we are told, "The Jews took up stones to stone him." They say to Jesus, "It is not for a good work that we stone you, but for blasphemy, because you, being a man, make yourself God."[8]

So the version of the confession in the *Gospel of Judas* represents yet a third telling of the confession, but now from the perspective of Judas. This perspective reverses the traditional reading of the story, casting it as a Gnostic parody. In this parody, the twelve disciples are gathered, and declare that Jesus is the "Son of *our* God."[9] The reference to "*our* God" is a reference to the Demiurge Ialdabaoth, to the lesser god, the creator and biblical god whom the Sethian Gnostics believed apostolic Christians worshiped. So the confession of the twelve disciples in the *Gospel of Judas* represents the confession typical of apostolic Christians ignorant of the very existence of the supreme God who dwells in the Aeonic Kingdom and is separate from Ialdabaoth, the creator and ruler of this world. The *Gospel of Judas* is pointing out apostolic Christian ignorance, and mocking it in a very sophisticated manner. When Christians confess that Jesus is the Son of God, the Sethians say, they do not realize their own ignorance and error – that they worship Jesus as the Son of the creator and biblical god, who is not the Father on high, but Ialdabaoth, through whom this universe came into being.

Of course, Jesus rejects the identification pronounced by the disciples in the *Gospel of Judas*. He expresses concern that the twelve disciples seem to be ignorant of what they have just said, since in the Sethian tradition Jesus is the Son of God the Father, not Ialdabaoth, who is the biblical God the disciples have referred to. He laughs at them, telling them that when they engage in eucharistic practices they are not worshiping the supreme God, but the lesser Demiurge. Jesus informs the twelve that they are so mistaken about his identity that none of them will ever be able to know him. Jesus says to them, "How do [you] know me? Truly I tell you, no generation will know me from the people who are among you."[10] He then mocks them, further challenging the "perfect" among the twelve to step forward. In this way, the story serves as a strong satirical attack as well as critique of the traditional Christian confession, implying that the apostolic Christians inadvertently and unknowingly worship Ialdabaoth when they confess Jesus as the Messiah and Son of God. Because of their ignorance, truly they will never confess or know the Son as he really is.

Judas' Subversive Confession

As in the traditional versions of the confession story, one of the disciples comes forward with the correct confession. In this case it is Judas rather than Peter or Thomas. Judas is the only one among the twelve who was "able to get up the courage to stand before him." So he stands up in front of Jesus, but turns aside his face because he is not able to look him in the eyes.[11]

What is the meaning of his posture and his aversion to looking directly at Jesus? This is the common language of deference and worship in early Jewish and Christian apocalyptic and mystical literature, applicable to angels who stand before God's throne in worship with averted eyes.[12] If an angel or human gazes directly on God's glory, the creature risks death. So worship of God in heaven is done either prostrate or upright but with averted eyes, faces covered by wings, or with intermittent peeks at the deity enthroned. Clearly, the posture of Judas suggests that he recognizes Jesus' divinity, but with a twist found nowhere in the apostolic Christian literature. Judas does not declare Jesus to be Yahweh's prodigy, but proclaims the Sethian confession, "I know who you are and where you come from. You came from the immortal Aeon of Barbelo, and the one who sent you, I am not worthy to speak his Name."[13]

The language here is similar to the confession story preserved in the *Gospel of Thomas*, where Thomas claims that his mouth is not able to say whom Jesus is like, a reference evoking the unpronounceable Tetragrammaton, YHWH.[14] In the *Gospel of Judas*, however, the unpronounceable Name is not Yahweh, the biblical god, but the great Father Aeon who, in Sethianism, is the God whom words are unable to express. In another Sethian text, a liturgy describes the indescribability of the Father Aeon in these terms: "We are not able to express him."[15]

Certainly this is a recognition scene with peculiar variations on the typical story. But then it is a Sethian midrash, so interpretative reversal and the revelation of hidden agendas are to be expected. Everything "traditional" in Sethian narrative is read upside down. The normal understanding of things is subverted. Nothing is as it seems. The point of this kind of reverse reading is for the Sethians to show up the ignorance of traditional interpretation, alongside the revelation of its true, esoteric meaning.

Typically, the heroic disciple is the one who recognizes and confesses Jesus. But does this mean that Judas is the heroic disciple in this confession scene? We should not rush to this conclusion, because the Sethians appear in their midrash to be reversing the story with sustained laughter. The traditional "good guy" Peter was known by the ancient Christians to have recognized Jesus as the Son of God and Messiah from the biblical narratives. But what if the Sethian interpretation is flipping this upside down? What if the focus of the story is on the fact that Jesus' disciples got the attribution wrong? Jesus laughs at them. Even more hilarious would be the fact that it was the unexpected "bad guy" who really got it right – the thirteenth disciple, Judas. In other words, I think that the Sethians who wrote the *Gospel of Judas* were pointing out that even Judas, the baddie of baddies, "got it" while the twelve couldn't; that even he, in all his wickedness, was more perfect than they! I cannot imagine a more subversive characterization of the twelve apostles, nor one more critical. Such a picture of the twelve disciples would have completely spoiled the authority of the twelve, upon which rested the faith of the entire apostolic church, a faith and a church that the Sethians wished to undermine and defeat.

Opposition to Apostolic Succession

Why would the Sethian Christians be so harsh on Jesus' twelve disciples? Why does the *Gospel of Judas* comment over and over again on their ignorance and identify them with worshipers of Ialdabaoth? Part of their subversive treatment of the apostles is interpretative. As we will see shortly, they are very careful readers of Gospels like Mark. They know that in these stories Jesus' disciples are both faithless and ignorant. Tertullian of Carthage tells us that the Gnostics regularly "brand" the twelve apostles, in particular Peter, with "the mark of ignorance" and "simplicity." He says that they also argue that the twelve apostles did not know everything, and so turn to Paul as their pride and joy for a fuller disclosure of knowledge and the revelation of God's mysteries.[16]

This position is quite offensive to Tertullian, who works very hard to try to save the credibility of the disciples in spite of the fact that the Gospel stories portray them as faithless and ignorant. He begins his justification of the twelve by calling his detractors' position "madness," and then asks, if the disciples were truly ignorant, why would Jesus ordain them to be teachers or always keep them by his side? Wasn't Peter the rock on which the church was built? Didn't he possess the keys of the kingdom of heaven? Didn't he have the power to loose and bind in heaven and on earth? Didn't John, the most loved of all the disciples, lean on Jesus' breast? Didn't Jesus point out to John alone that Judas would betray him?[17]

In the midst of this tirade against Christians who claim that the apostles were ignorant, Tertullian brings out his most powerful weapon, a doctrine that had been taking shape in the writings of the heresy-hunting church leaders, the doctrine called "apostolic succession." Apostolic Christianity, under the leadership of men like Irenaeus of Lyons and Tertullian of Carthage, instituted and defended this doctrine both to set their beliefs apart from those of other Christians like the Sethians, and to suppress them. They insisted that their own beliefs had been passed down to them through a chain of command which they traced directly back to the twelve apostles. Tertullian says that Jesus chose the "chief twelve," whom he "destined to be teachers of the nations." When Judas died, the eleven worked as teachers and quickly chose Matthias by lot as the "twelfth, in place of Judas." They all were given the Holy Spirit to work miracles, and were sent to every city in the world, preaching "the same doctrine of faith to the nations." In this way, Tertullian explains, there are "churches in every city, from which all the other churches, one after another, derived the tradition of the faith, and seeds of doctrine, and are every day deriving them." These churches Tertullian calls "apostolic," because they were "offspring" that could be traced back to the homogeneous and inspired message of the twelve apostles. In this way, "the churches, although so many and so great, comprise but the one primitive church, from the apostles."[18]

With this doctrine of apostolic succession in place, the apostolic bishops argued for the legitimacy and authority of their own beliefs, while denouncing the beliefs of other Christians. They railed against other Christians whose beliefs, they claimed, did not derive from the teachings of the twelve apostles. The apostolic Christians fabricated a bogus lineage for those they thought were "heretics," a lineage they traced back to the "father of all heretics," a certain Simon who is mentioned in Acts 8.9–24 as a Samaritan "magician." Bishop Irenaeus tells us that "all sorts of heresies derive their origins" from "this Simon of Samaria," a conceited, faithless man of the magical arts who invented the Simonian religion. Simon claimed that he was the incarnation of the Father on earth, sent to save the Spirit Mother, who had become trapped in the body of a prostitute, Helen of Tyre. Simon was the author of the "most impious doctrines" and from his movement "Gnosis" originated.[19] Irenaeus describes these "many offshoots of numerous heresies" and "a multitude of Gnostics" as springing up "like mushrooms growing out of the ground."[20]

The Sethian attack on the twelve apostles in the *Gospel of*

Judas is part of this bigger conflict, a conflict raging as a new religion was trying to define itself within an explosive atmosphere of increasingly sectarian truth-claims. Whoever wrote this Gospel operated from a perspective informed by highly literal interpretations of biblical stories about the twelve disciples and grounded in an apocalyptic cosmology in which Archons created and ruled the universe as opponents of the supreme God, Jesus' Father. To these Gnostic Christians, the apostles did not possess God's mysteries, but like the Archons remained ignorant of the truth. They were the leaders of the "human generations" that did not belong to the Aeonic Kingdom, admonished by Jesus in the Gospel of Mark as the "faithless generation" whom Jesus barely and only temporarily tolerated.[21]

The Twelve Disciples in the Gospel of Mark

What is so brilliant about this subversive narration of the confession story is that it is, in fact, incredibly faithful to scripture, particularly as Jesus' story is framed by the Markan author. According to the Gospel of Mark, the disciples are faithless and ignorant, failing to understand who Jesus is even though he has handpicked them as disciples.[22] He gives them special treatment, teaching them in private so that they may gain understanding that the crowds will never have.[23] But they do not get it. When he calms a storm at sea, they question who he is "that even wind and sea obey him." Jesus rebukes them for their "faithlessness." He says to them, "Why are you afraid? Have you no faith?"[24]

    A little later, after he multiples the fish and loaves to feed a crowd of five thousand people, it is said of the disciples, "They did not understand about the loaves, but their hearts were hardened."[25] As the narrative advances, Jesus warns them to "beware of the

leaven of the scribes and Pharisees." They completely misunder-
stand him, thinking that he is upset with them because they did not
have any bread. Jesus says to them in some exasperation, "Why do
you discuss the fact that you have no bread? Do you not perceive
or understand? Are your hearts hardened? Having eyes do you not
see, and having ears do you not hear? And do you not remember?
When I broke the five loaves for five thousand, how many baskets
full of broken pieces did you take up? ... Do you not yet
understand?"[26]

After Peter makes his confession according to the Markan
narrative, he blunders again, misunderstanding Jesus' prediction
that he must suffer and die. Jesus rebukes him as "Satan."[27] When
the disciples try to heal an epileptic boy, they are unable. He
immediately rebukes his disciples: "O faithless generation, how
long am I to be with you? How long am I to bear with you?"[28] – a
quote very much in line with the expressed opinion in the *Gospel of
Judas* about the disciples, including Judas.

Jesus tells the disciples in Mark that the one who will be first
must be last and servant of all. And yet the disciples spend their
time discussing among themselves who would be the greatest
among them. When Jesus asks them what they are discussing, they
fall silent.[29] Jesus again teaches the disciples that to be great means
to serve, and yet James and John tell Jesus that they want to sit at
his right and his left hand in glory. When the other disciples get
wind of this conversation, they become indignant, and Jesus has to
remind them all (because they still haven't got it!) that the first
among them must be a slave.[30] The repeated metaphor Jesus uses is
"Be like children." Yet, when the children come up to Jesus, the
disciples rebuke them, to Jesus' indignation.[31] In the end, the
disciples "all forsook him, and fled."[32] The only one who remains is
Peter, who three times denies knowing Jesus.[33] The disciples'

reputation is never redeemed, at least in our oldest manuscript versions of Mark, which end at 16.8. But, even in the longer ending of the Gospel of Mark, the disciples are chided by Jesus "for their unbelief and hardness of heart, because they had not believed those who saw him after he had risen."[34]

The author of the Gospel of Mark does not portray the twelve in anything near glowing terms. In fact, it can be argued fairly easily that Mark did not like the twelve and was arguing against their authority, trying to undermine it, as we find the Sethians doing in the *Gospel of Judas*. There is only one historical circumstance contemporary with the writing of Mark's Gospel (60–70 CE) in which such an extreme polemic against the twelve would make sense. It would only make sense as a Gospel written to try to destroy the credibility of the twelve disciples in the turf war between the mission of the Jerusalem church and the mission of Paul's churches.

The old Jerusalem church was controlled by Jesus' brother James and the twelve disciples. Its authority came from its reliance on the teachings of Jesus as they were remembered and dispersed by the disciples of Jesus. It was a Jewish movement, centered on getting the people of Israel ready for the coming of God's Kingdom and the immediate return of Jesus the Messiah as God's Judge. Anyone who converted to the movement had to become a full member of Israel. This meant circumcision for all male converts, changing the convert's diet to kosher foods, and teaching the convert how Jesus wanted him or her to observe the 613 laws given by God in the Torah.

Paul was not a disciple of Jesus. He never knew Jesus, at least the historical man. He persecuted the Christian Jews from the Jerusalem church, but eventually had a religious experience that converted him to the same faith he had persecuted. He had a personal ecstatic revelation from Jesus that led him to the life of a missionary. At first he was sponsored by the church in Antioch in western Syria, a northern hub of Jerusalem's mission. But Paul's message became radically Gentile in its orientation, and Paul went on to repudiate circumcision and kosher laws for converts. This did not go over well in Jerusalem. So Paul struck out on his own. As his letters tell us, he found the going tough, as he tried to compete with the disciples from the Jerusalem church who based their authority on their personal acquaintance with Jesus. Paul argues continually in his letters that the church communities should heed his own instructions, rather than the conflicting instructions from the Jerusalem mission. He calls himself an "apostle," basing his authority on his revelatory experience.

Was the author of Mark siding with the Pauline mission, attempting to undermine the credibility of the twelve? Was he trying to discredit the authority and teachings of the Jerusalem church, in favor of those of Paul, teachings that dispensed with kosher laws,[35] included Gentiles,[36] and focused on the universality of Jesus' atoning death, that Jesus the Messiah is a suffering and dying Messiah?[37] This seems very likely to me. The opinion expressed in the *Gospel of Judas* that the twelve disciples are clueless is not a fabrication of the Sethians who wrote it, but a robust (and literal) interpretation of the cynical storyline framed by Mark.

The Demons in the Gospel of Mark

What about those who actually "get it" in the Gospel of Mark? Who are they? The only ones in this Gospel who recognize Jesus are the demons he exorcizes, the Gentile Roman centurion at the foot of his cross, and the reader, who is taught that Jesus is an unexpected type of Messiah – one that must suffer, be rejected, and die "as a ransom for many."[38] Those who "get it" are not the twelve disciples, but the demons and the demon-possessed. They recognize Jesus' true identity as the Son of God long before Peter catches on. It is quite possible that Peter's recognition of Jesus in chap. 8 may have some connection to demon possession too, since Mark has Jesus rebuke Peter as "Satan" immediately following the confession itself:

> And Jesus began to teach them that the Son of Man must suffer many things, and be rejected by the elders and the chief priests and the scribes, and be killed, and after three days rise again. And he said this plainly. And Peter took him, and began to rebuke him. But turning and seeing his disciples, he rebuked Peter, and said, "Get behind me, Satan! For you are not on the side of God, but of men."[39]

We find in Mark 1.34 that "he healed many who were sick with various diseases, and cast out many demons. And he would not permit the demons to speak, because they knew him." Not only do the demons recognize him as the "Son of God" in Mark 3.11, but they fall down prostrate before him. Mark says, "And whenever the unclean spirits beheld him, they fell down before him and cried out, 'You are the Son of God.' "[40] This tendency to characterize the demons as those who recognize Jesus is epitomized in the story of the man possessed by a number of demons named Legion. When seeing Jesus at a distance, the possessed man ran up to him and worshiped him. "And crying out with a loud voice, he said, 'What have you to do with me, Jesus, Son of the Most High God?' " (Mark 5.6–7).

Were the Sethians casting Judas in this light? As a demon who recognizes Jesus' true identity when the rest of the disciples fail to? If Judas is to be understood in this sense, then the *Gospel of Judas* is a very sophisticated and subversive Gnostic critique of apostolic Christianity and its claim to knowledge and legitimacy by tracing its teachings back to the twelve apostles. If so, then these Gnostics were basing their critique on a literal reading of the storyline created by Mark. In the mind of the Sethians who wrote the *Gospel of Judas*, apostolic Christianity's reliance on the authority of the apostles for its legitimacy is ridiculous. Not only were the apostles ignorant (as the scripture says), but the only one who actually recognized Jesus was the disciple Judas, who was himself a demon!

So Judas' confession in the Gospel is far from demonstrative of his Gnostic stature, as the National Geographic team would have us believe.[41] Certainly in the *Gospel of Judas*, he appears to recognize the reality of Jesus' origin and nature while the other disciples do not, which is a challenge to the apostolic tradition of succession. But is this because the Sethians think Judas is a Gnostic? Or a man who is a demon or demon-possessed?[42]

CHAPTER 6

Judas the Demon

So who is Judas according to his Gospel? A perfect Gnostic? Or a demon? In my opinion, the text is unambiguous, preserving (and mocking) Judas' epithet "*daimon*," a common word in early Christian literature, used to identify maleficent beings, evil spirits, fallen angels, and the demonic host.[1] On p. 44 of the manuscript, Jesus calls Judas the "Thirteenth Demon." Judas says to Jesus, "Teacher, just as you have listened to all of the disciples (tell about their vision), listen now also to me. For I have seen a great vision." Jesus turns to Judas and laughs at him. Then he asks him, "Why do you compete (with them), O Thirteenth Demon?"[2] So the question for me is not *whether* Judas is a demon, but *what* demon he is.

The key to unlocking Judas' demonic persona is the number thirteen, which we also hear about a few pages later when Judas is complaining to Jesus. He is confused, wondering how he is supposed to benefit from Jesus' private teaching when Jesus has separated him from the holy Aeonic generation populating the upper Kingdom. He asks Jesus, "What is the advantage I received, since you have separated me from that generation?" In response, Jesus gives Judas three predictions about his future – that Judas will become the "thirteenth," that he will be "cursed" by the generations of the twelve apostles, and that he will become their ruler, "reigning" over the twelve generations.[3]

The Thirteenth Demon

Why the "thirteenth"? Is thirteen Judas' lucky number, as the National Geographic team has suggested, or is it still as unlucky as ever? [4] According to Sethian numerology and cosmology, thirteen is the most unlucky number one can be linked with, because it is the number associated with the demon Demiurge, Ialdabaoth, his assistant Archons, and his particular cosmic realm.

There are several standard Sethian texts from the Nag Hammadi collection that reveal this cosmic order. The Sethian *Holy Book of the Great Invisible Spirit* contains a section describing the creation of the heavenly realms surrounding the earth. At one point in the cosmogony, two angels are brought forth to rule Chaos and Hades. Their names are Saklas and Nebruel. These are not your typical "good" angels, assistants of God, but "bad" angels, assistants of the arrogant Ialdabaoth. So besides being called "a great angel," Nebruel is also called "a great *daimon*" with reference to his malicious power as an Archon. Saklas and Nebruel work together and create "twelve realms" surrounding the earth which they populate with twelve Archons, whose names are Athoth, Harmas, Galila, Yobel, Adonaios (a.k.a. Sabaoth), Cain, Abel, Akiressina, Yubel, Harmupiael, Archir-Adonin, and Belias.[5] Ialdabaoth, along with his assistants Saklas and Nebruel, resides above the entire cosmos in the thirteenth realm. So Ialdabaoth's nickname is "god of the thirteen realms."[6] Equally arresting is the Gnostic belief that the thirteen rulers of this world were "nailed" at the moment that Jesus' body was nailed to the cross, a point I will return to in a later chapter when the passion of the Christ is taken up.[7]

Another Sethian book that recounts this cosmology is the *Apocalypse of Adam*. In fact, the entire book is predicated on a universe consisting of "thirteen kingdoms" that are ruled by the Archons. The apocalypse describes each one of the thirteen kingdoms along with the attempts of the Archons to destroy the holy redeemer who journeys through the realms as he descends to earth and ascends back to his home.[8] A beautiful hymn celebrates his preservation in face of the wrath and hatred of his enemies the Archons.[9] These thirteen kingdoms ruled by the Archons are contrasted with the holy "generation without a king" above them.[10] The redeemer, "the great Illuminator," is from this upper Kingdom, this "great Aeon" or "foreign air." He resides in the Aeon above with a generation of people who have received his Name in baptism. These are the Gnostics, the ones who "have known God." They will "live forever," because they are not corrupted by "desire," nor have they colluded with the Archons and their schemes. They live eternally in the presence of the supreme God among his angels, who also dwell in this Kingdom Beyond.[11]

In *Zostrianos*, a Sethian revelatory book, the Sethian Gnostic initiate tells us about his initiation experiences, a series of revelations, baptisms and anointings that released his soul from his body, freeing it to journey past the cosmic realms into the upper Aeons belonging to the supreme God. In one of his first initiations, when his soul makes its way through the lower cosmic realms surrounding the earth, he says that he cast his body "upon the earth to be guarded by glories." Once this was done, he made his initial ascent up through the thirteen realms populated by the demonic Archons. He says that he "was rescued from the whole world and the thirteen realms in it and their angelic beings." He says that the lesser angels did not see his passage, but the Archon in each realm became disturbed because he noticed a "light cloud" moving through his territory.[12]

This is the same cosmology assumed by the *Gospel of Judas*. In the middle of the *Gospel of Judas* is a section in which Jesus reveals the truth about cosmology. Part of that revelation includes a recounting of the creation of the realms surrounding the earth and their populating with Archons. Out of a cloud immediately above the twelve realms appears an angel whose "face flashed with light" and who was "defiled with blood." Nebro or Nebruel is his name. He is equivalent to Ialdabaoth in this version of the myth. He is also called by the epithet "Apostate" because his allegiance is not to God the Father and Jesus the redeemer, but to the Archons, who populate the lower realms and war against the upper Aeon. Together, he and Saklas create six angelic assistants who help them produce "twelve angels in the heavens with each one receiving a portion of the heavens." The five angels who rule over the abysses (Chaos and Hades) are called [. . .]eth, Harmathoth, Galila, Yobel, and Adonaios.[13]

The first of these five names is probably a version of Athoth (Atheth), based on similar lists in other Sethian texts, not "[S]eth" as the National Geographic team has reconstructed it.[14] Moreover, in the National Geographic transcription, Atheth is given the abbreviated title *chs*. The team has assumed that this is an abbreviation for *christos*, the first (*ch*) and last (*s*) letters of the word, thus translating the line, "The first is [S]eth, the one who is called Christ." But this is nonsensical. Seth is never an Archon in these lists, nor is Christ ever made to be an Archon ruling over Chaos and Hades in the Sethian literature.[15] Rather, the abbreviated title, *chs*, is more likely from the Greek word *chrestos*, with the same first and last letters, but which means "the Good One." This is the epithet associated with Athoth in other Sethian texts.[16]

Judas' identity is tied up with the thirteenth realm. This realm belongs to the Archon who rules over the twelve heavens and the earth, Ialdabaoth. So Judas, with the nickname "Thirteenth Demon," is linked to Ialdabaoth and his realm. Judas is either a man operating under the influence of the demon Ialdabaoth, or Ialdabaoth's equivalent, perhaps understood to replace him or even merge with him one day. These expressions certainly do not indicate that he is a blessed Gnostic, a colossal overstatement if ever there was one on the part of the National Geographic team.

The Twelve Apostles Ridiculed

The *Gospel of Judas* is playful (in a sinister way) with Jesus' prediction that Judas' "star" will "[rule] over the thirteenth realm."[17] Jesus laughs at this in the Gospel. It is a mockery that befuddles Judas. Jesus responds, "I am not laughing [at you], but at the error of the stars."[18] Quite clearly, the Sethian Christians find it very humorous that Judas is locked into a fate that will elevate him to Ialdabaoth's throne as king and chief Archon of the thirteen kingdoms. I do not think, however, that it is so much Judas' assumption of Ialdabaoth's throne that the Sethians thought funny, but the prediction that Judas would rule over the twelve lesser Archons and the twelve lesser kingdoms. For them, Jesus' prediction that Judas will reign over the "twelve realms" is simultaneously sensible and subversive.[19]

What makes his elevation over the twelve Archons so subversive is that, in the *Gospel of Judas*, these lesser Archons are identified with the twelve apostles of the apostolic Christian churches.[20] These twelve apostles include Judas' apostolic replacement, who is mentioned only anonymously in the *Gospel of Judas*, but who is named in Acts as Matthias.[21] This comically (and conveniently) leaves Judas outside the apostolic twelve as the "thirteenth."

The Sethian identification of the twelve apostles with heavenly

Archons and cosmic realms in the *Gospel of Judas* was not a unique interpretation, for the *Gospel of Judas* is not the only Gnostic text to make this identification. In the *First Apocalypse of James*, from the Nag Hammadi collection, Jesus explains to James that there are not just seven heavens, as the scripture says, but seventy-two heavens, which are the realms of the twelve Archons. These Archons are armed adversaries of Jesus.[22] They are a "type" of the twelve disciples.[23]

Bishop Irenaeus of Lyons reports that another (and very different) group of Gnostic Christians, the followers of Valentinus, had identified the twelve apostles with a group of twelve Aeons within the Pleroma. This interpretation causes Irenaeus great discomfort because he says they located Judas among the twelve and claimed that he represented the type of suffering that the lowest Aeon, Sophia, experienced. Irenaeus considers this preposterous because everyone knows that Judas was not the twelfth disciple, but the "thirteenth." He also points out that characterizing Judas as the "twelfth" or the "thirteenth" doesn't support the Valentinian interpretation of him as a prefiguration of the Aeon Sophia, who was the "thirtieth" aspect of God produced.[24] Whether or not Irenaeus is correct in the identification of the Apostles with Aeons is questionable, since the second-century Alexandrian teacher, Clement, tells us that the famous Valentinian teacher, Theodotus, taught a cosmic identification. He said that "the Apostles were put in place of the twelve signs of the Zodiac, as birth is governed by the signs, so is rebirth (governed) by the Apostles.[25]

So the association of the disciples with supernatural beings is part of the wider Christian discussion taking place in the mid-second century when the *Gospel of Judas* was written. The numbers game appears to have been important, different sects of Christians making various connections between the disciples and numbers within their cosmological systems. The Valentinians followed a more apostolic interpretative trajectory, equating the twelve disciples with powerful aspects of the supreme God or replacements for the signs of the Zodiac. But the Sethians maintained their subversive interpretative tendencies, so that, like Judas, the twelve disciples do not fare well in the *Gospel of Judas*, as we already saw in the previous chapter.

After the disciples discover that Jesus visits a holy Kingdom, a holy generation, when he is not among them, they are confused. They have a hard time believing that there exists a generation "more exalted" and "holier" than they are themselves, a generation beyond the cosmic realms. Jesus finds their ignorance hilarious and tells them that anyone who is born from the cosmic realms cannot belong to the Aeonic Kingdom, a generation that is not ruled by the stars or the Archons of the lower realms.[26]

In order to show off, the twelve disciples report to Jesus a collective dream that they had one night. In the dream, they see a temple with an altar and twelve priests presenting sacrificial offerings on behalf of the crowd milling around. The sacrifices being offered are horrific in their eyes – child sacrifice topping the list! – and all are done in the Name of Jesus.[27]

Jesus then provides the disciples with his highly disturbing interpretation of their dream. The twelve disciples themselves are the twelve priests calling upon Jesus' Name. They themselves are the ones practicing child sacrifice and making other horrific offerings to the god Ialdabaoth, whom they serve. Truly "god" has received their sacrifices, he reassures them, but it is not the supreme God. It is the "Deacon of Error," the "Lord over the Universe," Ialdabaoth. And on the last day, Jesus tells them, they will be guilty of worshiping this false god, and leading astray the crowd milling around them, the countless generations of people to come.[28] Their dream is really their worst nightmare!

The Sethian opposition to the twelve disciples in the *Gospel of Judas* is part of the larger conflict of second-century Christianity coming of age in the midst of sectarian battles over Christian truth. The Sethians believed themselves to be the keepers of the keys to the Kingdom, and in these subversive stories in the *Gospel of Judas* they ridicule their opponents, particularly attacking the credibility of the twelve, upon which the apostolic churches based their faith. These stories continually remind the reader that the disciples are themselves part of the "faithless generation" that they lead. Following their teachings leads Christians astray and tricks them into worshiping the wrong god!

A Tragic Fate for Judas

Unlike the holy Gnostic initiate in *Zostrianos* who is able to ascend beyond the thirteenth heaven and the cosmic girdle into the Aeonic world above, Judas' best fate appears to be a final ascent to the thirteenth heaven, where he will replace or merge with Ialdabaoth and rule over the twelve disciples and the generations of apostolic Christians who have cursed Judas. Of course, this fate is one that Judas does not want, and he obstinately opposes it in his conversation with Jesus in the *Gospel of Judas*. And Jesus constantly insists that it will be his destiny.

For instance, following the twelve apostles' nightmare, Judas comes to Jesus begging him to listen to his own dream, thinking that its meaning suggests his inclusion in the Aeonic Kingdom. Judas tells Jesus that he saw in his dream the twelve disciples stoning him. He ran away and came to an immense house in which prominent people were living. Judas clearly understands the dream as a prediction – that he will be separated from the twelve disciples and join these prominent people one day. So in the Gospel, he pleads with Jesus, "Teacher, take me inside (the house) with these people."[29]

But Jesus responds, telling Judas that his star has led him astray, that the real meaning of the dream is a nightmare – that Judas will be locked out of the house. What Judas saw, according to Jesus, is the place that God has reserved for the saints, the Gnostics themselves, who will "stand forever" beside the holy angels. Those of mortal birth are not worthy to enter that house, and this includes Judas. Jesus reminds Judas that he has erred in his interpretation, led astray by his star, and states again that Judas' destiny will be as the chief ruler over the twelve realms.[30]

But the discussion doesn't end there. Judas becomes irate and verbally lashes out at Jesus, "Teacher, enough! At no time may my seed control the Archons!" Jesus then says to him that not only will he rule over the Archons, but he will "grieve much more" because he has seen the Aeonic Kingdom and its holy generation in his dream.[31] This is just as Jesus had predicted earlier in the Gospel where he told Judas that when he went to the Kingdom, he would lament terribly.[32]

This part of the conversation ends tragically for Judas. He demands to know what advantage he has received from having this dream, since Jesus has separated him from the generation of Gnostic saints. Jesus repeats, "You will become the Thirteenth, and you will be cursed by the other generations, and you will rule over them." Jesus ends this portion of the conversation with the definitive declaration, "You will not ascend to the holy generation."[33]

After this, Jesus says to Judas that he has now been told everything. He asks him to gaze upward and see a luminous cloud, the stars surrounding it, and the star in the ascendant, a star that he identifies with Judas'.[34] Then, the text says, "Judas lifted his eyes. He saw the cloud of light and he entered it."[35] Who does "he" refer to? The actual identity of the one who ascends into the luminous cloud is unclear because the text is so fragmentary here. It could be Jesus, or it could be Judas. If it is Jesus, then Judas never goes anywhere in the *Gospel of Judas*. Throughout the text he is "on the ground" so to speak. He has a dream vision, but no ascent.

But if it is Judas who ascends into the luminous cloud, the cloud appears to be a fixture of this cosmos, not the Aeonic Kingdom. Why? Because it is described as a cloud within the universe surrounded by stars. Because of its stellar location, it is impossible for it to be identified with one of the luminous clouds within the upper Aeons beyond the cosmic girdle. Stars are fixtures of this cosmos, never the transcendent Aeons.

So whose cloud is it? In Sethian tradition, this particular stellar cloud is the cloud where Ialdabaoth lives, enthroned in the thirteenth heaven. This is standard Sethian cosmology and is even reflected earlier in the *Gospel of Judas* when Nebro-Ialdabaoth's six assistants, including Saklas, come into being in a cloud.[36] As we saw, they create twelve angels to rule each of the twelve heavens below them. This luminous cloud is their operation's headquarters and exists in the thirteenth heaven.

This cloud of Ialdabaoth is quite prominent in Sethian texts from the Nag Hammadi collection. The cloud is fashioned by Ialdabaoth's mother Sophia in order to hide the monster she had created. The *Apocryphon of John* relates that the monster was so ugly that "she cast it away from herself, outside that place, that no one of the immortal ones might see it, for she had created it in ignorance. And she surrounded it with a luminous cloud, and she placed a throne in the middle of the cloud that no one might see it except the Holy Spirit, who is called the mother of the living. And she called his name Ialdabaoth."[37] *On the Origin of the World* relates that Ialdabaoth "sits upon a throne of light; a great cloud covers him."[38] In the *Holy Book of the Great Invisible Spirit*, Oroiael calls forth an angel to rule Chaos and Hades. When he does so, "the cloud, being agreeable, came forth in the two monads, each one of which had light. [. . .] [the throne] which she had placed in the cloud [above. Then] Saklas, the great [angel, saw] the great demon [who is with him Nebr]uel." Together they set up the twelve spheres below them and populate the spheres with twelve Archons.[39]

So if the "he" refers to Judas, it appears that his ascent is not all that glorious, but would be just what to expect given the basic features of the Sethian reinterpretation of Judas' story. Judas will join Ialdabaoth in his cloud becoming assimilated with Ialdabaoth in some way. There Judas will mourn his awful fate. The *Gospel of Judas* is unrelenting on this point – Judas may not want the fate he has, a fate that ties him to Ialdabaoth, but he is unable to change it.

At one point in the Gospel, Jesus says to Judas that he will tell him the "mysteries of the Kingdom" not so that he can go there, but so that he can grieve greatly.[40] This corrected reading of the Coptic found in *The Critical Edition* does *not* suggest an ascent to the Kingdom for Judas. Rather it assumes that Jesus has other reasons for giving Judas the revelation. We must consider the placement of this prediction within the entire narrative cycle of the Gospel. Where does it occur? Before Judas' dream, before he goes to the house of prominence and sees the people living there. Judas thinks this means that he will be allowed inside. But Jesus tells Judas that he is mistaken – that what he saw was the Kingdom from which he will be excluded. At the conclusion of this dream-and-interpretation sequence, Jesus flashes back to his earlier statement, saying again to Judas, "Behold, I have told you the mysteries of the Kingdom."[41] This suggests to me that the earlier statement, that he would grieve much, is nothing more than a foreshadowing of Judas' dream when he "sees" the Kingdom. But his hopes of entry are dashed with Jesus' words, and Judas begins to lament his tragic fate, wanting to know what good it is to have this knowledge if he is to be separated from the holy generation.[42]

The Revelation of Sethian Mysteries

The argument between Jesus and Judas quickly turns into a revelatory monologue followed by a couple of questions from Judas to clarify the fate of the human generations. In this section of the *Gospel of Judas*, Jesus finally reveals the "mysteries of the Kingdom" to Judas that he promised to do pages earlier when he told Judas, "I shall tell you the mysteries of the Kingdom."[43] These mysteries are details about how the Sethians understand the universe to have come into being and how it is structured.

Why would Jesus want to tell this to Judas? Does Jesus consider Judas a Gnostic? Or is something more complicated at work? If we analyse the flow of the narrative, it is very clear that these Sethian teachings are sandwiched between two declarations from Jesus that Judas' fate ties him to the thirteenth realm and Ialdabaoth.

46.18–47.1	Jesus answered, saying, "You will become the Thirteenth, and you will be cursed by the other generations and will rule over them. And in the last days, they < *missing line* > to you. And you will not ascend to the holy [generation]."
47.1–55.9	Jesus instructs Judas about the Sethian world
55.10–20	"And your star will [rule] over the thirteenth

Aeon." Afterwards, Jesus laughed. [Judas said,]
"Teacher, [why are you laughing at me?"]
[Jesus] answered, [saying,] "I am not laughing
[at you], but at the error of the stars, that these
six stars wander with these five warriors, and
they all will perish along with their creations."

This framing of the mystery teaching suggests to me that Jesus
shares the Sethian information with Judas not because Jesus
considers Judas to be a Gnostic, but to explain to Judas who
Ialdabaoth is, where he came from, and what his role in the universe
is. Essentially Jesus is teaching Judas the identity and location of the
Archons Judas is bound to, in one final attempt to show Judas that
his fate is mixed up with them. Jesus' revelation is meant to tell Judas
exactly who Ialdabaoth is, what alliances Judas will be making when
he betrays Jesus, and where he can expect to go afterwards. Jesus is
trying to demonstrate Judas' awful fate to him.

This is why the revelation ends with a final discussion about
the destiny of the various generations of people. Those generations
which are attached to the twelve realms, Jesus teaches, remain
under the influence of the stars or Archons controlling those
realms. And their leader? Well, Jesus repeats, it will be none other
than Judas who will be the ruler of the thirteenth kingdom. In the
end, Judas and all his kingdoms will perish, a thought that makes
Jesus laugh.[44]

Gnostic Baptism and Rebirth

Why does Judas become locked into this awful fate? This is the real
mystery of the *Gospel of Judas* in my opinion. It is possible that we
are witnessing a Gnostic doctrine of predeterminism, since not all

human spirits are created equal in Sethianism. Judas' spirit was likely identified with the counterfeit spirit created by Ialdabaoth and given to the human generations by Michael, a spirit that remains subject to the stars and Fate no matter the circumstance.[45] Although the Gospel is fragmentary, I think the manuscript hints at the importance of Gnostic baptism in overcoming fate for those people who have divine spirits granted them by Gabriel.[46]

In the Sethian tradition the baptismal ceremony was called the "five seals." This ceremony appears to have consisted of a series of multiple baptisms in the name of a series of water angels who were responsible for the "living water." The names of these water angels are Michar, Micheus, Seldao, Elenos, Zogenethlos, Mnesinous, Yesseus Mazareus Yessedekeus, Yoel, and Barpharanges.

The Gnostics believed that these rituals were brought down by the Redeemer during his descent, as indicated, for instance, in one of their hymns recorded by Bishop Hippolytus of Rome: "Possessing the seals I will descend, all the Aeons will I pass through, all secrets will I reveal, the forms of the gods will I disclose and the hidden things of the holy way, which I have called Gnosis, I will impart."[47] This revelation of baptismal knowledge is quite pronounced in the Sethian *Apocalypse of Adam*, which concludes, "This is the hidden knowledge of Adam, which he gave to Seth, which is the holy baptism of those who know eternal knowledge through those born of the world and the imperishable illuminators, who came from the holy seed: Yesseus Mazareus, [Yesse]dekeus, [the living] Water."[48]

What did the baptisms do? The Sethian *Holy Book of the Invisible Spirit* tells us that Gnostic baptism alters the initiate's place in the cosmic drama, defeating the cosmic and Demiurgic grip on the person's spirit. In this way, it re-enacts the cosmic battle at the crucifixion between Jesus and "the powers of the thirteen Aeons", who nailed Jesus to the cross but could not seize his spirit.[49] The "five seals in the spring baptism" guarantee that the initiate will "by no means taste death."[50] What this means is that the soul was freed from the Archons and the fate of their stars. This baptismal theology is highlighted by Clement of Alexandria, who quotes the Valentinian Gnostics as saying, "Until baptism, Fate is real, but after it the astrologists are no longer right. The washing doesn't liberate by itself, but also the knowledge of who we were, what we have become, where we were or where we were placed, where we hasten, from what we are redeemed, what birth is, what rebirth is."[51]

Something similar appears to me to be the subject of the discussion on pp. 42 and 43 of the *Gospel of Judas*. Jesus tells the disciples that each one has his own star.[52] The text breaks off here, but the coherent fragments that follow the break suggest that his speech included a discussion of the everlasting uncorrupted Gnostic generation which has been baptized in a spring that waters God's Paradise.[53] I think it is quite likely that the 17 missing lines on p. 42 addressed the ineffectiveness of apostolic Christian baptism in overcoming fate and one's connection with one's star, given the criticism of the sacramental practices of apostolic Christianity throughout the *Gospel of Judas*, as well as the immediate context, which aligns each disciple with a star.

The same discussion appears to have taken place on pp. 55 and 56 of the Gospel, although it too is fragmentary. Jesus tells Judas that he is not laughing at him, but at the deceitfulness of the stars and how they and their creations will all perish.[54] Then Judas asks a question about baptism, wanting to know what good comes of being baptized in Jesus' name (as the apostolic churches do) if they will all perish anyway? He says, "So what will those who have been baptized in your Name do?"[55] Jesus responds, "Truly I say to you, this baptism [. . .]."[56] This phrase is at the bottom of the page. Of the first ten lines on the next page, eight are wholly illegible or missing altogether. The first comprehensible line is in the center of the page, a discussion that appears to criticize apostolic sacramental practices, including the eucharistic meal as a re-enactment of Jesus' sacrifice.[57] So I think it very likely that the missing portion of the page included a discussion of the ineffectiveness of apostolic baptism in overcoming fate, and the effectiveness of Gnostic baptism in doing so. I also think it is quite appropriate to assume that Judas has not undergone Gnostic baptism because he remains connected to his star.

What we do know from the manuscript is that Judas is separated from the everlasting generation and his soul remains linked with the Archons and the fate of his star. Judas' tragedy is used by the Sethian author to criticize and mock his apostolic brothers and sisters, who do not themselves realize that the demonic disciple they curse is in fact the one who made possible their atonement, a criticism I find frighteningly profound.

From the perspective of Judas Iscariot, the *Gospel of Judas* is a pitiful tragedy. Judas is linked to the cosmic system in such a way that he becomes inseparable from Ialdabaoth and his evil plans against Jesus. He is tied to Ialdabaoth's realm and his cloud of operations, the thirteenth Aeon, and Ialdabaoth's persona as the King of the Archons. He is identified with the arch-demon ruling over his twelve assistants, a coincidence in number that was exploited by the Sethians to expose the illegitimacy of apostolic authority. The apostolic church's claims to knowledge handed down from the apostles is ridiculous once the apostles are recognized as the lesser Archons, ignorant of God and powerless over their arrogant ruler, whose evil plan to kill Jesus is executed.

CHAPTER 7

Judas the Sacrificer

The *Gospel of Judas* climaxes near its end, at the moment when Jesus prophesies that Judas will be the one who sacrifices him to the Archon Saklas. At this moment Judas becomes the "Apostate," the apostle turned renegade, operating to advance the Archonic plan. The Sethians who wrote this Gospel insist that Judas' part was more than a simple kiss on the cheek. What Judas did was the most evil thing he could do. By sacrificing Jesus to Saklas, he was instrumental in making operative the Archons' destructive plan. Jesus tells him this after a lengthy (and unfortunately fragmentary) monologue about the sacrifices that the disciples will make, all of which are "evil." Then he says to Judas, "You will do worse than all of them, for the man that clothes me, you will sacrifice him."[1]

Jesus goes further than this, predicting that Judas will be a successful apostate who carries out this most evil of deeds. "Already your horn has been raised," Jesus says, "and your wrath kindled, and your star ascended, and your heart has [...]."[2] The meaning of the first phrase, "Already your horn has been raised," is particularly telling, since it appears in the Psalms to refer idiomatically to military victory. When the conqueror has been victorious in battle, he signals this by blowing his battle horn triumphantly in the wake of his enemies' defeat.[3]

The phrase "your wrath kindled" speaks of Judas' motivation. In the *Gospel of Judas*, Judas is portrayed as a disgruntled disciple, one who does not like to hear what Jesus has to tell him, especially about a destiny he wishes not to have. So the reader gets the impression that his apostasy, his involvement in Jesus' sacrificial death, has been motivated by an anger that he bears against his teacher.

But his anger against Jesus is really misplaced, since it is his "star" that is causing him all this trouble, a point that Jesus repeats in his conversation with Judas. Here Jesus' reference to the ascendancy of Judas' star ("and your star ascended") is astrological language indicating that Judas' actions are determined, that Judas does not have a choice in the matter. His actions will be instrumental in handing Jesus over to the Archons. Even though the Archonic plan backfires when Jesus' powerful spirit slips through their hands, and their grip on human souls and destinies is destroyed, this does not appear to lessen Judas' personal involvement in the evil and traitorous plot or his alignment with the Archons.

Judas' role in the Passion story is presented to us in the *Gospel of Judas* in such a way that his actions are understood to have a supernatural dimension, to reflect a larger mythology of conflict and war between the supreme God and the Archons led by Ialdabaoth, Saklas and Nebruel. This represents Sethian mentality, where what happens on earth is only the tip of the iceberg. Earthly activities are sponsored by the spiritual world, so that what happens here only happens here because something larger and more profound is happening in the world of the supernatural. This spiritual activity has been hidden from humans in such a way that only through revelation given by a descending Aeon from the supreme God can the true meaning of the earthly occurrence become known.

The paradigm here is not a "mirror image" paradigm as it is in the very different Valentinian Gnostic tradition, where earthly activities are shadows or imperfect reflections of the activities of the upper Aeonic world. In Sethianism, human beings are participants in a supernatural drama. This drama always involves an action by the upper Aeons to redeem their lost light, and a counter-action by Ialdabaoth and his assistants to stop the redemption. The stories involve intrigue, suspense, and trickery on the part of both parties as they engage in a primordial and historical war over the human spirit. Since some of the action occurs on earth in historical time, the war involves not just Aeons and Archons, but also human beings. So human beings unknowingly become engaged in this supernatural drama.

This is what the *Gospel of Judas* is about – Judas' involvement in this supernatural drama. Judas is not a human actor betraying a human Jesus as a good friend, collaborator, or confidant. Rather, as we have seen, he is aligned with the Archons and demons who rule this world. The Archons form a powerful army warring against the Father above, wishing to kill Jesus before the Father can implement whatever plan of his own he may have been contriving against them.

The Gnostic Passion of Jesus

This portrayal of Judas is reminiscent of other Gnostic texts from the Nag Hammadi collection, texts that talk about the hidden drama of the Passion and crucifixion when Jesus' spirit separates from his dying body. In the *Second Treatise of the Great Seth*, it is described as an event of supernatural proportions.[4] It all began when a great Power came forth out of the "house of the Father of Truth"[5] and descended into "a bodily dwelling" as Jesus' soul.[6] The Power had to descend in disguise so that the Archons would not recognize the descending god and corrupt him with their wickedness. So the Power constantly alters its shape, changing from form to form, assuming the likeness of the Archonic beings it encounters along the way. In this manner, its passage goes unnoticed, and the Power remains undefiled by the descent.

What is this story really about? It is about the descent of Jesus' soul from the Aeonic world above to the earthly world below. The story is told in such a way as to emphasize the uniqueness of Jesus' soul – unlike the average soul, which experiences corruption as it descends and becomes embodied, Jesus' soul, a superpower, was not corrupted as it came into the world.

As the story continues, we find out that the Archons, although not recognizing the descent of this Power, do appear to recognize that something is up. As the Power becomes incarnate as Jesus, it takes the place of a soul already embodied, and this process disturbs the Archons.[7] In the confusion, Adonaios, the fifth Archon and one of the rulers of Chaos and Hades, suggests, "Let us seize him," while other Archons caution that "The plan will certainly not materialize."[8] They do not know what trick the Father is up to and appear confused about what action, if any, they should take. In the end, the Archons in control of Hades decide to act before the Father's plan can be implemented completely. In so doing, they hastily crucify Jesus, an action which they think, in their ignorance, will put an end to any trick the Father has set in motion in Jesus.

But their plan turns out to be their downfall. Jesus' soul does not succumb to them as they planned because, being incorruptible and without error, it cannot die like other human souls. The Power that is in Jesus says, "I did not die in reality but in appearance."[9] "I was about to succumb to fear" but did not, so "my death which they think happened, (happened) to them in their error and blindness, since they nailed their man to their death."[10] Everything that the Archons do to Jesus – the punishments and beatings, forcing him to drink gall and vinegar, crowning him with thorns – in reality they do to themselves. Even Jesus' cross is not carried by Jesus, but by Simon the Cyrene, "who bore the cross on his shoulder."[11]

A similar description of Jesus' death on the cross is found in the late second century Sethian text, *Melchizedek*. He is crucified in the third hour, after which he rises from the dead. He is strong, engagin the Archons in battle. "You have [prevailed over them, and] they did not prevail over you," we read, "[and you] endured, and [you] destroyed your enemies."[12]

So what *really* happens at the moment of Jesus' death? According to the *Second Treatise of the Great Seth*, his spirit leaves him and rejoices "in the height", laughing at the ignorance and error of the Archons, who thought they were tricking the supreme God by crucifying Jesus. Jesus' spirit has the last laugh because the Archons are not only tricked, but trick themselves. The release of the powerful spirit of Jesus means their own downfall. So his spirit says, "I was laughing at their ignorance. And I subjected all their powers."[13] By nailing Jesus' body to the tree, and fixing his hands and feet with "four nails of brass," they are really killing themselves, not Jesus.[14] Why? Because Jesus' spirit cannot be fettered by the Archons. It is released from his body, "their man," and breaks out of the cosmic girdle. A great trembling seizes the earth and the souls of the dead are released. They ascend and unite with Jesus' spirit, which opened up a path for them to the world above.[15]

This Gnostic interpretation of the passion is referred to in other texts, such as the *Apocalypse of Peter*, which states that, although the Archons crucified Jesus' body, they were unable to hold onto "the living Savior" who stands joyfully watching and laughing at their blindness and lack of perception. Jesus' body in reality was Jesus' substitute and, by killing it, the Archons released "my incorporeal body," "the intellectual Spirit filled with radiant light."[16]

What about Judas' role? What do the other Gnostic texts have to say about it? The best window into his role in Gnostic texts is found in the *Concept of Our Great Power*. According to this text, Jesus' earthly ministry and teaching disturbed the Archons, a comment similar to what is recorded in the *Second Treatise of the Great Seth*. The Archons become angry and decide to try to catch him and hand him over to one of the Archons overseeing Hades, known as Sasabek in this particular presentation of the myth. So these Archons sought out one of Jesus' disciples, Judas, and possessed him – as the text relates, "a fire took hold of his soul." Their possession causes Judas to betray Jesus, who is then delivered to the ruler of Hades by the Archons themselves for nine bronze coins. Sasabek tries to seize Jesus, but cannot because "he found that the nature of his flesh could not be seized." He shouts in astonishment, "Who is this? What is it? His word abolished the law of the realm. He is from the Logos of the power of life!"[17] And so Jesus is victorious over the ruling Archons, and ascends to the Father. His ascent carves out the passage upward out of the cosmic girdle, opening the way for other souls to follow. His defeat of the Archons begins the process of the end of the world, the dissolution of the cosmos and the Archons' control over human destinies and souls.[18]

Gnostic Criticism of Sacrifice and Atonement

The *Gospel of Judas* assumes this type of Gnostic interpretation of Jesus' Passion and Judas' involvement in his betrayal. Judas' action is not understood as a straightforward this-worldly affair, but as involving a supernatural cast and agenda. Judas is aligned with the Archons who rule this world, an evil host battling the Father and his Aeons. Judas' spirit is the Thirteenth Demon, carrying out the plan of Ialdabaoth and his cronies as their leader.[19] By betraying Jesus, Judas offers Jesus' body as a sacrifice to Saklas, a sacrifice more evil than any that the other apostles would ever make:

> Truly [I] say to you, Judas, those [who] offer sacrifices to Saklas
> < *several missing lines* > everything that is evil. Yet you will do
> worse than all of them. For the man that clothes me, you will
> sacrifice him.[20]

By framing Judas' sacrifice of Jesus alongside that of the other apostles, who sin by also offering evil sacrifices to the Archons,[21] the Gospel goes a long way toward criticizing and mocking apostolic interpretations of Jesus' death in sacrificial terms. This criticism condemns apostolic interpretations of the crucifixion, which held that Jesus' death atoned for sins. To the Gnostic Christians who wrote the *Gospel of Judas*, this interpretation was hideous because it assumed child sacrifice – that a father would and should kill his own child. So heinous a crime was this, so immoral, that the Sethian Christians could not stomach it, and so they accuse the twelve disciples of engaging in child sacrifice (among other crimes they considered hideous), and understand Judas the demon as the one who initiated it.

Further, they reason, if Judas is a demon who makes the sacrificial offering, who does he make the offering to? Surely not to the supreme God, since he does not work for him. Judas must have made the sacrifice to the Archons with whom he colluded, handing him over to one of their leaders, Saklas. This means that the worship of the apostolic Christians does not save them, because any sacrifice was made to the Archons, not God the Father. The apostolic Christians do not realize it, but they are worshipers of Ialdabaoth, directing their praises to him, the "Deacon of Error," the "Lord over the Universe," especially when they gather together to partake of the sacrificial elements at the eucharistic table.[22]

So when the twelve apostles gather together and prepare the offering of bread, Jesus' laughter echoes loudly. The *Gospel of Judas* says that when he approached his disciples who were seated together, he saw that they were giving thanks over the bread. "He laughed." His reaction provoked the disciples to respond, "Teacher, why are you laughing at [our] eucharist? We have done what is right."[23] Jesus says to them, "I am not laughing at you. You do not do this by your own will, but by this, your god [will] be worshiped."[24]

What is going on here? Certainly this is not a historical narrative representing Jesus' actual engagement with his disciples. What it is, however, is something of equal value. It is a fictionalization of an authentic historical dialogue in which the Sethian Christians were engaged with the apostolic Christians. Jesus' laughter is the laughter of the Gnostic Christian. The apostles' assertion is the assertion of the apostolic Christian. Jesus informs the apostles that when they partake of the elements, what they are really doing is worshiping Ialdabaoth, the god to whom Judas will offer Jesus as a sacrifice. The apostolic Christian argues to the contrary, that the practice of the eucharist is rightly done. The Gnostic Christian responds that the practice is deceptive, done under the influence of Ialdabaoth's will, and only serves to worship him, not the supreme God, Jesus' Father.

This is quite a clever argument, I think, given the Sethian universe. It makes sense that Judas the demon would be working for (or as!) Ialdabaoth. This means that the apostolic Christian argument that Jesus' death atones for sin is marginalized and loses its power, as it is really a sacrificial act made by the demon Judas to the demon Ialdabaoth. Any re-enactment of that sacrifice – when bread is blessed during the eucharist ceremony – is a fraudulent act, serving only to give praise to the ruler of this world and strengthen his grip on the world and human beings.

The Devil's Ransom

This sophisticated critique appears to have concerned apostolic Christian thinkers. What we find in the Christian literature after the *Gospel of Judas* was written is an increased interest in Judas' role in Jesus' death. Before the mid-second century, Judas is rarely mentioned in the literature and when he is, it is a mere repetition of the "facts" about him from the Gospels we find in the New Testament or fanciful embellishments of these "facts." Satan possessed him, he was a repentant traitor, and he killed himself, says Bishop Ignatius of Antioch.[25] Papias of Hierapolis, writing in the early second century in a five-volume exposition he called *The Sayings of the Lord Interpreted*, knew a dialogue between Jesus and Judas "the betrayer." In this dialogue, Judas did not believe a prophecy that Jesus had made about an abundant harvest at the end of time. Jesus replied, "Those who come into those times will see," a reply which suggests that Judas will not be part of the harvest.[26] Papias also knows a story that appears to be a simple expansion of some of the details of Judas' death recorded in Acts. Judas was an obese man whose body was so swollen with impiety that he could not cross the road without being hit by a chariot, his bowels gushing out on impact.[27]

In the late second century, interest in Judas increases, not so much in the number of references, but in terms of trying to interpret his actions. Judas' actions appear to have become a liability for the apostolic Christians. How could you trust a religion whose leader was betrayed by his closest follower? Jesus must have been a bad "general" who could not control his subordinates, or one who produced such ill will that his subordinates committed mutiny. This was the perspective of Celsus, a Roman philosopher in the second century who wrote a scathing attack on Christianity.[28] Celsus goes on to offer another possibility. Maybe the impiety of his disciples should be traced to Jesus himself, who was their example, since, after "banqueting with God," Judas "became a conspirator." Otherwise Celsus writes, "God himself plotted against the members of his own table, by converting them into traitors and villains!"[29]

The famous Christian teacher Origen of Alexandria would have none of this and responded to Celsus' criticisms by quoting Psalm 109.1, "Do not be silent, O God of my praise! For wicked and deceitful mouths are opened against me." Origen claims that this psalm is a prediction about Judas, from the lips of Jesus. If its contents are carefully observed, Origen argues (rather weakly I think), we will see that Judas himself was responsible for his traitorous actions, not Jesus.

Tertullian of Carthage finds himself in a confrontation with teachings about Judas that he traces to Marcion, a Christian in the mid-second century who, as noted in Chapter 1, formed his own churches and created the first New Testament, whose contents included a revised version of the Gospel of Luke and ten letters of Paul. Marcion believed that Yahweh, the god of the Old Testament, was a completely different god from the "Unknown God" Jesus preached and Paul taught about in Acts 17.23: "For as I passed along, and observed the objects of your worship, I found also an altar with this inscription, 'To an unknown god.' What therefore you worship as unknown, this I proclaim to you." Marcion says that the Old Testament god is proven to be deceitful and a fraud because he knowingly chose Judas as Jesus' betrayer. Marcion then suggested that, because of this, Judas should be granted impunity.[30]

Tertullian finds this outrageous, and he works hard to prove Marcion wrong on this point (and hundreds of other points – his book against Marcion is five volumes long!). His main defense is a saying he lifts from Luke's version of the Last Supper, when Jesus predicts that someone among them will betray him: "Woe to that man by whom the Son of Man is betrayed!" If Judas were to be granted impunity, surely Jesus would not have used "woe." This is not an "idle word," Tertullian writes, and suggests that Judas will be punished for the sin of treachery he committed.[31]

What I find most intriguing in the late second century is the rise of an interpretation of Judas which locks him into the Devil's own conspiracy. Tertullian, following Luke and John's portrayal of Judas as possessed by Satan or *a* devil, says that "*the* Devil entered into him." He describes the process as a process of possession – that Judas kept his own soul, but it was augmented by the Devil himself.[32] He claims that the Devil instigated Judas to betray Jesus,[33] out of "desperation and excessive malice with which the most abandoned slaves do not even hesitate to slay their masters. For it is written in my Gospel that 'Satan entered into Judas.' "[34]

Origen of Alexandria says that Judas accepted the Devil *fully* into himself, as it is written that after the supper, "Satan entered into him."[35] Why could the Devil send a "fiery dart" into Judas' soul and take complete possession of him? Because Judas' soul was already being eaten by spiritual gangrene, a wickedness hidden deep within him. Wasn't Judas' concern for the poor in the Gospel story really a cover to hide his thievery?[36]

What is astonishing about Origen's early third-century discussion, however, is the way in which he then uses this link between Judas and the Devil to think of God's bigger plan of redemption in terms of a ransom paid to the Devil, an idea rooted in the Gospels and Paul.[37] Both Justin Martyr and Irenaeus in the mid-second century had been fostering theories of redemption "by his blood and the mystery of the cross," theories that Jesus saved human beings by "earning" us through his suffering and death.[38] Justin thought that it was by God's will that Jesus should "take upon himself the curses of all, for he knew that, after he had been crucified and was dead, God would raise him up."[39] Irenaeus says that human beings have been redeemed "by his own blood in a manner consonant with reason." Jesus "gave himself as a redemption for those who had been led into captivity." Irenaeus never comes out and says that human beings are captive to the Devil, but he intimates this, saying that the "apostasy" tyrannized us unjustly, alienating us from God, who really owns us. Jesus righteously turned against that "apostasy" and redeemed his property, an atonement through his blood by "giving his soul for our souls, his flesh for our flesh."[40]

Origen's contribution to this theory is one that looks to me unique and, I think, responsive to the Gnostic criticisms lodged against these apostolic theories of atonement. Origen ties Judas tightly to the Devil and the theory of ransom in what appears to me an attempt to resolve this earlier problem articulated by the Gnostic Christians in the *Gospel of Judas* – that a demon is responsible for Jesus' death and any atonement he may have brought about was by and for the Archons who rule this world. No, Origen counters, it is God who uses the demons. Origen develops his argument by referring to Paul's statement that *God*, not the demon Judas, was the one responsible for sacrificing Jesus – God "spared not his own son, but delivered him up for us all."[41]

What did Origen make of this statement in light of the Gospel stories about Judas, which insist that it was Judas who did the delivering? Origen thinks this must mean that God delivered Judas to the demons and that Satan then used Judas to deliver Jesus into the hands of men. Even more significant is the fact that Origen thinks this ploy by God is a trick to defeat the demons, particularly the Devil, the Power of Death.[42] Jesus was "delivered into the hands of men" by "the prince of this age," the Devil, who earlier had tempted Jesus with kingship over worldly kingdoms. Because Jesus was able to rise from the grave, the Devil's own kingdom and power was destroyed – including the great enemy "Death" – when this transaction was made.[43] The redemption of the sinful dead was transacted as a purchase from the Devil. The price? Jesus' blood.[44] The Devil accepted the purchase price, but was unable to keep hold of Jesus, who was more powerful, and rose from the dead. So the Devil was cheated out of his ransom.

Origen's systematic theory addresses the problems that the Gnostic Christians had raised about the apostolic church's doctrine of atonement – that the sacrificer was a demon. Versions of Origen's theory became quite popular in medieval Christianity. Pope Gregory the Great, in fact, actually argued that the Devil had acquired "rights" over fallen humanity, rights that God had to respect. The only way for human beings to be released from his domination was if the Devil exceeded the limits of his authority, which would mean that he forfeited his rights over humanity. This could only be achieved if a man free of sin were to enter the world, yet appearing as a normal sinful man. The Devil would not notice what was happening until it was too late. Jesus' humanity was the "bait" and his divinity was the "hook." The Devil, like a great sea monster, snaps at the bait, and is hooked before he realizes it.[45]

The atonement was (and still is) a cherished interpretation of Jesus' death among Christians. Nonetheless, it is an interpretation that came after the fact of his death. Because of this, the interpretation didn't align exactly with the way in which the Christian story remembered Jesus' death – that a demonic Judas was the one who actually made it happen.

The Sethian Gnostics in the *Gospel of Judas* pointed out the obvious problem with this. If Jesus' death really was a sacrifice made by God for the purpose of salvation, why would a demon be the instrument? And why would Judas be cursed for his involvement?

The apostolic solution struck them as humorous because they felt that it showed up the ignorance and ineffectiveness of the apostolic faith. Judas was a demon, and the god who put out Jesus' warrant was Ialdabaoth. Judas collaborated with him, and together they brought about Jesus' sacrifice, which was nothing less than apostasy and murder. The sacrifice was a sacrifice to Ialdabaoth, so all eucharistic offerings serve only to worship and extol him.

Their critique does not seem to have gone unnoticed by the apostolic Christians, since their leaders begin to rethink the Judas story in the late second and early third centuries. Origen, particularly, takes on the task of reshaping the story, tying Judas tightly to the Devil. Judas' involvement in Jesus' death wasn't the Devil's idea. It was God who turned Judas over to the Devil, selecting Judas, whose soul was already filled with spiritual gangrene. The ploy was part of tricking the Devil to kill Jesus, so that God could ransom the souls of the dead with Jesus' blood. But in the end the Devil was cheated out of the ransom because he could not contain Jesus' powerful spirit.

The end of Origen's story is not so different from the Gnostic story. Granted, for the Gnostics, the truth about Jesus' death was not to be found in his bodily and bloody sacrifice. But it was the moment when his powerful spirit was released and conquered the Powers who tried to subdue him. The Gnostic interpretation of his death is victory over Death and the Powers who enslave the human spirit. On this point, I think Origen and the Gnostics were on common ground.

CHAPTER 8

An Ancient Gnostic Parody

What does the *Gospel of Judas* really say? If we follow the story-line from beginning to end, what it means is different depending on your perspective. If you are Judas, it is a story of tragedy, of a human being who became entangled in the snares of the Archons who rule this world. If you are an apostolic Christian, it is a story of ridicule, a representation of your faith as based on faithless apostles and a demon-sponsored atonement. If you are a Sethian Christian, it is a story of humor, of laughter at the ignorance of Christians not in the know.

The Narrative in Brief

The *Gospel of Judas* is an ancient Gnostic parody that begins on p. 33 of the Tchacos Codex with Jesus' criticism of the eucharist as it is offered by the twelve disciples. Jesus shows the disciples how ignorant they are, since they don't realize that the eucharist is a ceremony in which Ialdabaoth is worshiped, not the supreme God. On p. 34, he immediately chastises them for not knowing who he really is, and challenges the perfect among them to step forward and brave the truth. The twelve are further belittled when on p. 35 even Judas, the demon, is able to step forward and announce Jesus' real identity. Is Judas, the wickedest of all men, more knowledgeable than they? Because Judas has braved the challenge, Jesus promises him that he will tell him the mysteries of the Kingdom, but warns him (foreshadowing Judas' later dream) that Judas will lament greatly. Then Jesus leaves.

On p. 36, Jesus appears again to the disciples, who express concern about where Jesus goes when he is not in their presence. When Jesus tells them about the holy generation of which they are not a part, they can't believe it. It isn't possible, they declare to Jesus, for another generation to be holier than they themselves. Jesus laughs and criticizes them again, explaining to them that they are from the human generation and will be unable to associate with those from the holy generation.

The disciples wish to show Jesus that he is wrong, that they have great holy visions. So on pp. 37 and 38, they relate to Jesus a communal dream that they had the previous night. They say that they saw Jesus and a great temple with an altar. Twelve priests were sacrificing children on the altar, invoking Jesus' Name. The images in the dream clearly troubled them and so they wait for Jesus to tell them the dream's meaning. Jesus offers them his interpretation of the dream on pp. 39 and 40. Jesus tells them it was no dream vision, but their worst nightmare. For the disciples were the priests making the sacrificial offerings, and although they may have invoked Jesus' Name, the god who heard them and accepted the offering was none other than Ialdabaoth. The disciples are committing terrible sins against the supreme God by leading Christians astray, and on the last day they will be judged guilty.

This is followed by several pages of instructions that Jesus gives to the disciples and Judas (pp. 41–44). These pages are very fragmentary, but he appears to be teaching them all about the fate of the different generations of people. The human generations are connected to the stars and their fates, while the people of the holy generation have overcome their fates because they have washed in the spring that waters God's paradise. All humans will die, body and soul. What survives is the spirit of those from the holy generation.

Judas then relates to Jesus on pp. 44–45 his own dream, wishing to prove to Jesus that he is better than the ignorant twelve, that he is part of the holy generation. Jesus laughs at his efforts, and calls him by name the "Thirteenth Demon." But Jesus listens as Judas recounts his dream. In it he saw the twelve pick up stones and throw them at him. He runs away to a great house filled with important people. He thinks that his dream means that he will be separated from the twelve and join the holy generation. So he asks Jesus to let him into the house.

Jesus refuses, telling Judas that his star has led him astray, that his interpretation is erroneous. Only saints can enter the house of the holy generation and live with the angels who dwell there. So Jesus says that he has told Judas the mysteries and taught him about his fate as King over the twelve cosmic realms.

This leads to a confrontation between Judas and Jesus on p. 46. Judas wants no part of the fate that Jesus is predicting for him. So he flatly refuses: "Teacher, enough! At no time may my seed control the Archons!" Jesus tries to settle him down by explaining it to him again – that seeing the Kingdom and all its generation is the cause of great lamentation. Judas demands to know what advantage it is to be taught by Jesus and see the Kingdom in his dream if Jesus has separated him from the Kingdom. Jesus answers by telling Judas that he will become the Thirteenth, that he will be cursed by the other generations, and that he will be King over them. In the last days, they will all perish. Judas will not ascend to the holy generation.

This opens up into many pages of instructions about the structure and genesis of the Sethian world (pp. 47–55). Jesus tells Judas this information in order to explain to him how the lines are drawn – who Ialdabaoth is, who he is at war with, what territories he controls, what his relationship to human beings is, and so forth. This is meant to give Judas a map so that he knows that he is in collusion with the Archons, who are working against the supreme God and his Aeons. At the conclusion of these instructions, Judas is again laughed at by Jesus, who explains that Judas is the "thirteenth Aeon" whose star will rule the cosmos. In the end, the stars at war will perish along with their creations. Judas asks about the benefits of apostolic baptism, but Jesus' answer cannot be reconstructed given the fragmentary nature of the manuscript at this point.

On p. 56, Jesus condemns the sacrifices that the twelve offer to the Archon Saklas, their god, and explains how evil this is. Then he says to Judas that Judas will do more evil than all of the disciples, because he will sacrifice Jesus himself. He quotes from scripture to prove that his prediction is prophecy already fulfilled, and that there is nothing that Judas can do to prevent this action. The Archon will be destroyed, and the holy generation exalted. Then on p. 57, he shows Judas his star in the ascendant, indicating that his fate is accomplished. Judas sees a luminous cloud and "he" enters it. The cloud appears to me to be Ialdabaoth's, given the stars surrounding it, grounding it in the cosmic atmosphere. On p. 58, the story turns to its final scene, a recounting of the beginning of Mark 14, the moment when the Sethians thought that Judas conspired with the high priests and scribes to hand Jesus over to them.

A Voice in the Present

The *Gospel of Judas* is an unfamiliar story, from its descriptions of a laughing Jesus to its bitter feelings about the twelve disciples to its orgasmic conception of the universe. Oddly, the one aspect of the story that is probably most familiar to us is Judas, the demon-possessed man who betrayed Jesus! The Gospel's unfamiliarity results from the fact that Sethian Christianity did not survive into the modern world. It was actively suppressed and forgotten by apostolic Christians, who became the keepers of the keys to the Kingdom.

The recovery of the *Gospel of Judas*, one of those welcome accidents of history, has given the Sethian Christians another hearing, in another time, in another place, to another audience. Much of what these Gnostic Christians have to say in this troubling but perceptive Gospel I find still relevant today, providing material for reflection.

Much of the *Gospel of Judas* is about authority. Where should we turn to for authority? To our traditions? To our institutional leaders? To our religious scriptures? To ourselves? What happens when our traditions, our leaders, or our scriptures do not agree with our consciences? What happens when they conflict? For the Sethian Gnostics, there was only one answer to this question. We must follow our consciences, that internal spirit, that piece of God within us. Why? Because that inner spirit is our truth. We are the fallen God embodied, they thought. There cannot be a higher authority than the internal one.

The great worry for them was the external authorities who, like the Archons, wished to trap us and impose their ignorance and arrogance upon us by suppressing our ability to think for ourselves and to act out of our own consciences. So the *Gospel of Judas* objects to Christians blindly relying upon their church's teaching without reasoned reflection. Sethians especially questioned the doctrine of apostolic succession, which taught that the mainstream Christian faith with its creeds and rituals was passed down from the mouths of the twelve apostles to bishops like Irenaeus of Lyons and leaders like Tertullian of Carthage.

Their critique of apostolic succession itself was quite clever, because it in turn questioned scripture and its interpretation as external authorities. They held the scriptures up to a mirror, asking the apostolic Christians, have you ever really looked at the Gospel of Mark, one of the scriptures and foundations of your faith? Have you ever really read it or heard it preached? If you had, the Sethians said, you would have seen that the twelve disciples are ignorant and faithless and that even when Jesus gives them special teaching they still don't get it. In fact, the twelve disciples are so blind and their hearts so hardened that even the demons are smarter than them, since at least the demons recognize Jesus for who he really is. Why would anyone, the Sethians asked, wish to claim their faith to be based on teachings passed down from ignorant men? Shouldn't we rely instead on our own reason and experience, our own inspiration and revelation, to unlock the truth?

Even more troubling for the Sethians, however, was the apostolic teaching that Jesus' death was a sacrifice of atonement made by God to wash away the sins of humanity. The idea that God would commit infanticide was so morally reprehensible to the Sethian Christians that they almost could not fathom it. I think the writing of the *Gospel of Judas* was a Sethian act of conscience. They felt that they could no longer stand by and watch Christians institutionalizing God's sacrifice of his Son in eucharistic ceremonies.

So abhorrent was this practice to them that they turned to the Judas story and created a parody to expose the problems with the doctrine of atonement and to ridicule the eucharist. They did this by organizing the story of Judas around a nightmare sequence where the twelve disciples witness twelve priests committing horrific acts of sacrifice on an altar in Jesus' Name. Jesus tells them that they are those priests, and that their horrific acts of sacrifice are committed on the altar of the rebellious god Ialdabaoth. Why Ialdabaoth's altar and not God's? Because, the Sethians reasoned, the person who committed the worst act of sacrifice, the killing of Jesus, was Judas, a demon himself. What demon was he? The "Thirteenth," the convenient nickname for Ialdabaoth in the Sethian stories! So the sacrifice he brought about must have been a sacrifice planned, caused, and committed on behalf of Ialdabaoth by Ialdabaoth. Judas was a demon working for a demon. This conclusion completely negated the efficacy of the eucharist and made the ritual so ridiculous that Jesus laughs.

These Sethian barbs were not ignored. The apostolic Christians felt them. And they responded by re-creating the doctrine of the atonement in such a way that Judas the demon was no longer a problem. At the beginning of the third century, we hear the great theologian of early Christianity, Origen of Alexandria, come to the rescue. He sets forth a theology of ransom that begins as God's trick on the Devil. God selects Judas, a man with a soul already corrupted by evil, and delivers him to the demons. The Devil uses Judas to betray Jesus to the hands of men who crucify him. So God gives his Son to be killed by the Devil so that Jesus' blood will be God's ransom money. The Devil accepts the money and fulfills his end of the bargain, giving over to God the sinful dead. But what the Devil doesn't realize is that Jesus' spirit is a power much stronger than him, so it could not be contained and rose from the dead. In this way God was able to cheat the Devil and save humankind.

As fascinating as this revision of the Judas story is, I find it profound that Origen's whole revision depends upon the final element, that Jesus' spirit was released at his death. Because of its power, it could not be confined and so the Devil loses. This is the common ground between our two dissenting forms of Christianity, and it is the point of the Gnostic *Gospel of Judas*. The "good news" of the *Gospel of Judas* is about Jesus, that Judas the demon only killed Jesus' body when he made his horrific sacrifice to the Archons. Jesus' death is really about his spirit which, when released, conquers the Powers that rule the world. So Jesus says toward the end of the Gospel that the Archon will be destroyed![1] His destruction is what makes it possible for the fallen God trapped within us to return home. This is how the rupture in God is repaired. This is how God, at last, saves himself.

Epilogue

When I attended the first international academic conference on the *Gospel of Judas* at the Sorbonne in October 2006, I had breakfast with a French-Canadian colleague from the University of Laval. Professor Louis Painchaud told me that he thought the "good" Judas is a modern myth, a rehabilitation of the evil Judas, a consequence of our collective guilt for the horrors that anti-Semitism has wreaked over the centuries, and our reappraisal of Jewish and Christian relationships in the wake of World War II.

I hesitated. Could this be? Are we as a modern society collectively trying to dodge the fact that deeply embedded within the Christian story is an anti-Semitic narrative? Are we trying to alleviate our guilt and responsibility for the centuries of senseless and needless violence against Jews by removing the responsibility for Jesus' death from Judas?

Early Jesus Films

What has run through my mind since that conversation with Professor Painchaud are the films that I frequently show in my cinema class, "Jesus at the Movies." How sinister the portrayals of Judas are prior to the Second World War. In Sidney Olcott's 1912 black-and-white film, *From the Manger to the Cross*, a bleak and ugly Judas actively reaches out for the morsel of bread that Jesus holds, and then he dramatically leaves the supper scene to wander down a dark street alone. His motivation is greed, accepting payment from a council of Jewish leaders for his traitorous act. After the kiss in the garden, he runs back to return the blood money to those who hired him because he is afraid of Jesus' power, which he witnessed when Jesus healed a man's severed ear. There is no remorse, only the intense desire to escape the wrath of one more powerful than he.

Judas' motivation for greed is compounded with a love triangle fifteen years later in Cecil B. DeMille's famous (and sexy) film, *The King of Kings*. Judas is identified in a subtitle as "The Ambitious" disciple who joined Jesus' movement because he expected Jesus to become a king. Because of his intimate friendship with Jesus, Judas expects to get glory and money once Jesus is crowned. Judas is so loyal to Jesus that he even neglects his beautiful courtesan and girlfriend, Mary Magdalene, to spend his time with Jesus instead. Judas decides to betray Jesus only after Jesus refuses to allow him to crown him as King on the Temple stairs. The dramatic scene of the payment of the money emphasizes his intense disappointment and greed – each of the thirty pieces of silver drops with a thump on the table as a bitter and pensive Judas watches with the audience. At the supper, he feigns to eat the bread from Jesus' hand and refuses to drink from the cup passed around, clearly concerned and afraid that Jesus has found him out. Judas witnesses Jesus' beating and the crucifixion, which torments him to hang himself at the moment of Jesus' death with the very rope that had bound Jesus when he was scourged.

Jesus Films in the Fifties and Sixties

After the Second World War, the Jesus film returns to the silver screen in a much more playful form, and images of Judas' motivation and his responsibility for Jesus' death shift dramatically. Perhaps the most dramatic shift can be seen in Henry Koster's film, *The Robe*, which was based on the popular novel by Lloyd Douglas published in 1942. Koster was born Hermann Kosterlitz in Berlin. When Hitler rose to power, Kosterlitz, a Jew, fled to Budapest and eventually altered his name. His film is fascinating in that it explores in great depth the motivations and feelings of Jesus' killer. But it is not a story about Judas. It is a story about a fictitious Roman tribune, Marcellus Gallio, who drives the nails into Jesus' hands and feet, and then lives to regret it. Judas has been completely erased.

The 1961 film *King of Kings*, produced by Samuel Bronston, presents a complicated story based on a Gospel harmony and a fabricated plotline in which Barabbas is the leader of a Jewish rebellion engaged in overcoming their Roman oppressors. Bronston carefully attaches images of the Holocaust to the Roman colonizers, setting up a contemporary commentary on the story of Jesus. How does Judas fare? Rather well. He is attached to Barabbas' rebel movement as Barabbas' friend and he wishes for Jesus to become their prophetic leader. The audience sympathizes with the oppressed rebellious Jews led by Barabbas and Judas against the "Nazi" Romans.

Judas' role is to convince Jesus to join the rebellion as their prophet even though Judas knows that Jesus speaks only of peace. Barabbas tells Judas that peace in Jerusalem can only be won by the sword. But Judas tries to convince his friend that Jesus will be forced to come round after he preaches at the Temple and the crowd proclaims him King. Without Judas' knowledge, however, Barabbas sets up a revolt at the same time that Jesus is scheduled to preach at the Temple, to use the moment for his revolutionary cause. It all backfires when the Romans massacre the rebellious crowd in the courtyard outside the Temple.

Judas blames himself for the senseless and needless slaughter, feeling betrayed by Jesus, who did not come to their aid. And this sets into motion his own betrayal of Jesus to Caiaphas the High Priest. No money is mentioned or exchanged because Judas' motivation is not "evil." It is moderated. A combination of misunderstanding, guilt and hopelessness drives him to Caiaphas. The audience's pity for Judas grows when he watches Jesus drag his cross up Golgotha. As he sees Jesus being put on the cross, he is distraught. Barabbas is beside him and has an epiphany that Jesus is dying in his place. Barabbas wonders why he should do that, since Barabbas never did anything for him. Then the audience hears Jesus' voice, saying, "Forgive them." All this is too much for Judas, who realizes that he has misjudged Jesus, so he commits suicide and dies at the same moment as Jesus.

Jesus Films in the Seventies and Eighties

Norman Jewison's 1973 release of *Jesus Christ Superstar*, with its singing Jesus, had Judas as its main focus. Andrew Lloyd Webber, the man responsible for the musical, said that the basic question underlying the rock opera was whether or not Judas Iscariot had God on his side,[2] a question also posed by Bob Dylan in his famous 1963 song "With God on Our Side,"

> In a many dark | hour, I've been thinkin' about this, | that Jesus Christ was betrayed by a kiss. | But I can't think for you. | You'll have to decide, | whether Judas Iscariot had God on his side."

In this musical, the traditional Passion story is told in a very untraditional way, from the perspective of Judas. Right from the beginning of the movie, Judas has his doubts about his friend Jesus.

Judas is highly rational, highly modern, questioning the man behind the "myth." He sings that Jesus has started to believe that he is God, to believe that the things people are saying about him actually are true. He is stunned and worried for his friend, worried that all the good Jesus has done will soon be forgotten because Jesus has begun to matter more than what he has to say. Judas pleads for Jesus to listen to him, to remember that he always has been his right-hand man. He is concerned that Jesus will disappoint and hurt his followers when they discover that he is just a man, not God, the boy from Nazareth, not the new Messiah. Judas screams in fear that the crowd will crush them. He yells a warning to Jesus, to listen to him.

Once Judas decides to betray Jesus, he is reluctant and does not want to be damned forever. He explains to the priests Annas and Caiaphas that he came because he felt he had to, because he is the only one who can see that Jesus cannot control the movement any more. Even more stunning is his statement that Jesus would approve. Not only has Judas' motive been cast as "good" in the sense that he is motivated out of worry for his friend's life and reputation and concern for his own nation; he thinks that the Romans will destroy Israel to deal with any riot caused by disaffected crowds once they learn the truth about Jesus.

What is really new in this movie's approach to Judas is that Judas thinks Jesus approves of his motivation and actions. Judas continues singing, as he falls to the floor, that Jesus would not mind that he has come to the priests. Judas insists that he has no thought of his own reward. He really did not come to them of his own accord. What should Judas do with the money he will receive? Caiaphas tells him to think of the things he could do with the money. He could give it to a charity. Or to the poor. Caiaphas notes his motives. He notes his feelings. He tells Judas that this is not blood money. It is only a fee, and nothing more. The chorus brings the scene to a close, congratulating good old Judas on a job well done.

Judas' death lyrics follow these same lines. He acknowledges that everyone will blame him for Jesus' death even though he acted for Israel's good. He saved Israel from suffering, but was saddled with Jesus' murder. He has been spattered with innocent blood, and demands to know from God why he was chosen to commit God's crime. He accuses God of murdering him. The lyrics create a Judas who misunderstood, who believed himself to be destined by God to save Israel by killing Jesus. The scene ends by saying goodbye to poor old Judas.

Martin Scorsese was intrigued by Judas' motivations as well. His 1988 film *The Last Temptation of Christ* is based on Nikos Kazantzakis' novel, first published in 1955. In his film, Judas steps forward in amazingly new ways. From the beginning he is Jesus' friend. He is a member of a Jewish zealot movement and sharply chastises Jesus for building wooden crosses for the Romans. Judas meets Jesus again in the desert on a mission to assassinate him in order to put an end to his collaboration with the Romans. They have a heated conversation in which Jesus convinces Judas to join him instead, to support him emotionally as he preaches about God. Jesus wonders if God has sent Judas to follow him rather than to kill him. Judas decides to go along with Jesus until he can understand what Jesus is up to, but he warns Jesus that if he strays even a little, he will kill him.

And so the plot emerges as a tale of two friends, one willing to kill the other if things go wrong. And things do go wrong. Eventually Jesus realizes that he is going to die, that he must die to fulfill the prophecies of Isaiah. He tells this to Judas, who becomes frustrated and says to Jesus that every day he has a different story.

One day it is about love, another day it is about the ax being laid to the root of the tree, and now today it is about needing to die. The scene shifts and Jesus is urgent with Judas, insisting that he has to die on the cross. He explains to Judas that their actions will bring God and man together. Jesus must be sacrificed to God. Judas becomes agitated and distraught as Jesus continues, drawing Judas to his own demise, insisting that Judas is the one that will make salvation possible. He says that Judas will bring this about, that he will kill Jesus, that God will do this through his actions. Jesus sets up the plot, telling Judas that he will go to Gethsemane, and that Judas will bring the soldiers there to find him. The scene ends with a remarkable exchange between the two friends. Judas is broken and asks Jesus whether, if they switched places, Jesus could betray his master. Jesus replies that he would not be able to do that, which is why God gave him the easier task.

Our modern consciousness appears to need a "good" Judas. We have generated plot after plot, character after character, story after story, to exonerate Judas, to figure out his motivations, to make him our friend and hero. Is the initial interpretation of the *Gospel of Judas* by the National Geographic team part of this larger modern fantasy, this modern myth of a "good" Judas that we have communally constructed in the wake of the ravages of World War II?

I don't pretend to know the answer to this question. But this I do know. Dante's raw Catholic image of the evil Judas, whose fate in the jaws of Satan is a living hell, is far closer to the description of the thirteenth disciple in the Gnostic *Gospel of Judas* than the hero in Scorsese's film or National Geographic's documentary will ever be.

Further Reading

The Gospel of Judas

Cockburn, Andrew, "The Judas Gospel," *National Geographic Magazine,* **May 2006, 78–95.** This is National Geographic's story of the year, perhaps of the past century. Mr. Cockburn, a National Geographic author, writes an overview of the discovery and restoration of the *Gospel of Judas* in fine journalistic style. Beautiful photographs by Kenneth Garrett grace the pages.

Ehrman, Bart D., *The Lost Gospel of Judas Iscariot: A New Look at Betrayer and Betrayed* **(Oxford: Oxford University Press, 2006).** Professor Ehrman discusses his own involvement in National Geographic's project to analyse the *Gospel of Judas* along with the tale of the discovery of the Gospel. He describes the contents of the Gospel and its relationship to the New Testament Gospels, suggesting that it presents a unique view of Jesus, the twelve disciples, and Judas, who is the only one who remains faithful to Jesus even to his death.

Evans, Craig A., *Fabricating Jesus: How Modern Scholars Distort the Gospels* **(Downers Grove, Ill.: Intervarsity Press, 2006).** Included in the back of this book is a brief appendix, "What Should we Think about the *Gospel of Judas?*" Evans mentions his own involvement on the National Geographic team and the recovery of the text. He outlines those contents of the Tchacos Codex yet to be published. This is followed by a short description of the contents of the Gospel and its meaning, where Evans gives his opinion on the perspective of the Church Fathers – that the gospel honored Judas because it was written by a Gnostic who revered all the "evil" men in the scriptures. These villains, like Judas, were only "evil" in the eyes of Yahweh the lesser god because they worked for the God of light in his war against Yahweh. So Evans understands the authors of the *Gospel of Judas* as Gnostics who believed that the villains were the good guys.

Gathercole, Simon, "The Gospel of Judas," *Expository Times* **118.5 (February 2007), 209–15.** In this brief article, Professor Gathercole summarizes the early literature about the *Gospel of Judas*. His analysis is based on the English translation published by National Geographic. He discusses the manuscript and its origins, gives a running interpretative narration of the contents of the Gospel, and highlights its significance in terms of Gnosticism and Christianity in the second century. He concludes that it does not tell us anything about the historical Jesus or Judas.

Gathercole, Simon, *The Gospel of Judas: Rewriting Early Christianity* **(Oxford: Oxford University Press, 2007).** This book includes Dr. Gathercole's English translation of the *Gospel of Judas* and a running commentary on the text. He has also made new translations of all the ancient testimonies about Judas and his Gospel. He provides an analysis of the relationship between this Gospel and the New Testament Gospels, and sets the *Gospel of Judas* in the context of a bitter dispute between Gnosticism and mainstream Christianity.

Head, Peter M., "The *Gospel of Judas* and the Qarara Codices: Some Preliminary Observations", *Tyndale Bulletin* **58 (2007), 1–23.** This readable academic article comments on the nature, history, date, and importance of the *Gospel of Judas* by paying attention to where it was found, what other books were found with it, and what other literature is in the same book as this Gospel. His paper cautions against saying too much about the interpretation of the *Gospel of Judas* until scholars can check the reconstruction of the Coptic, something that can only be done when complete photographs are published. He says that once this has been done, alternative interpretations and translations should be produced.

Kasser, Rodolphe, Meyer, Marvin and Wurst, Gregor, with additional commentary by Bart D. Ehrman, *The Gospel of Judas* (Washington, DC: National Geographic, 2006). The original publication of the English translation of the *Gospel of Judas*, made by Professors Kasser, Meyer, and Wurst, in collaboration with François Gaudard. It includes chapters of commentary on the story of the Tchacos Codex (by Kasser), *Judas* as a typical Gnostic text and alternative vision of Judas (by Ehrman), early mentions of the *Gospel of Judas* by the Church Fathers (by Wurst), and *Judas* as a Sethian Gospel (by Meyer).

Rudolphe Kasser and Gregor Wurst, *The Gospel of Judas, Critical Edition: Together with the Letter of Peter to Philip, James, and a Book of Allogenes from Codex Tchacos* (Washington D.C.: National Geographic,

2007). This is the first critical edition of the Tchacos Codex. It contains full-color photographs of the original papyrus manuscript pages in addition to Kasser-Wurst's Coptic transliteration and English translations. The book contains supplemental introductions, indices, and interpretative essays.

Krosney, Herbert, *The Lost Gospel: The Quest for the Gospel of Judas Iscariot* (Washington, DC: National Geographic, 2006). Herbert Krosney, an investigative journalist, traces what can be known about the discovery, recovery, and restoration of the *Gospel of Judas*. Includes a brief foreword by Bart Ehrman and an epilogue by Marvin Meyer.

Pagels, Elaine and King, Karen L., *Reading Judas: The Gospel of Judas and the Shaping of Christianity* (New York: Viking, 2007). This book contains Professor King's own English translation of the *Gospel of Judas*, followed by a brief running commentary. The other chapters are written collaboratively by Professors Pagels and King. These chapters attempt to contextualize Judas within the milieu of early Christian persecution and martyrdom, suggesting that the Christians who wrote this Gospel were condemning church leaders who were encouraging their flocks to die as sacrifices to God.

Perrin, Nicholas, *The Judas Gospel* (Downers Grove, Ill.: Intervarsity Press, 2006). In this pamphlet Nicholas Perrin provides us with a brief history of the discovery of the *Gospel of Judas*. He gives an overview of the contents as a second-century Gnostic Gospel. He argues that the text has little historical value as an account of Jesus and Judas. Rather, its value comes from what it reveals about Gnostic alternatives to what Perrin understands as "authentic" Christianity.

Porter, Stanley E. and Heath, Gordon L., *The Lost Gospel of Judas: Separating Fact from Fiction* (Grand Rapids: Eerdmans, 2007). Professors Porter and Heath write against the sensationalism that has surrounded the initial publication of this Gospel by setting the *Gospel of Judas* in its historical context. They provide the reader with a brief history of Judas from New Testament texts and from the writings of the Church Fathers. They discuss one Gospel as a Gnostic philosophical text, and question its authenticity, defending the New Testament Gospels as true Christian Gospels.

Robinson, James, *The Secrets of Judas: The Story of the Misunderstood Disciple and His Lost Gospel* (San Francisco: Harper, 2006). Professor Robinson discusses what can be known about the historical Judas from the Bible and other ancient Christian texts. He recounts the story of the discovery of the *Gospel of Judas* and its sensationalistic release by

National Geographic, criticizing the way in which the publication of the text has been handled.

Wright, N. T., *Judas and the Gospel of Jesus: Have we Missed the Truth about Christianity?* **(Grand Rapids: Baker Books, 2006).** Bishop Wright argues that the *Gospel of Judas* tells us nothing about the historical Jesus or the historical Judas. Its rehabilitation of Judas in this second-century text cannot be linked to the real Judas, who betrayed Jesus. He thinks that the publication of this Gospel is part of a scholarly agenda to find an alternative Jesus, which has another sensationalistic life in popular literature like *The Da Vinci Code* – the agenda of financial profit.

Second-Century Christianity

Bauer, Walter, *Orthodoxy and Heresy in Earliest Christianity* **(Philadelphia: Fortress Press, 1st edn. 1934, 2nd edn. 1971).** This is the book that inaugurated the new quest for Christian origins within the diversity of early Christianity. Professor Bauer studies different geographical locations and the literature produced by the early Christians in these areas. He argues that the initial form of Christianity was "heretical" by later standards. The orthodoxy that comes to define Christianity did so at a relatively late date through the Church councils that began to be held. A classic.

Bettenson, Henry, *The Early Christian Fathers: A Selection from the Writings of the Fathers from St Clement of Rome to St Athanasius* **(Oxford: Oxford University Press, 1st edn. 1956, 2nd edn. 1969).** This is a standard edited collection of excerpts from the writings of the early Church Fathers. It is organized to provide a convenient overview of the development of Christian thought, life and worship during the ante-Nicene period.

Ehrman, Bart D., *Lost Christianities: The Battles for Scripture and the Faiths we Never Knew* **(Oxford: Oxford University Press, 2003).** This book shows how certain second-century Christianities were suppressed, reformed or erased by the mainstream Christians, those whom Professor Ehrman calls "proto-orthodox." Out of this battle emerged the New Testament canon as well as a standardization of Christian faith. This allowed the other Christianities to be denounced as heretical and purged. He covers several key second-century texts and groups including the *Gospel of Peter*, **the** *Acts of Paul and Thecla*, **the** *Gospel of*

Thomas, the *Secret Gospel of Mark*, Ebionites, Marcionites, and Gnostics.

Ehrman, Bart D., *Lost Scriptures: Books That Did Not Make It Into the New Testament* **(Oxford: Oxford University Press, 2003).** This is the companion volume to *Lost Christianities*. It contains English translations of fifteen Gospels, five apocryphal Acts of the Apostles, several apocalypses and secret books, and a number of canon lists. Each is preceded by a brief introduction by Professor Ehrman.

Hultgren, Arland J. and Haggmark, Steven A., *The Earliest Christian Heretics: Readings from Their Opponents* **(Minneapolis: Fortress Press, 1996).** A collection of excerpts from the Church Fathers about the second-century heretics. These include a few quotations from the heretics themselves, as well as second-hand descriptions written by the Church Fathers. Excerpts cover Simon Magus, Nicolaus, Menander, Cerinthus, Carpocrates, Saturninus, Basilides, Cerdo, Apelles, Valentinus, Marcion, Montanus, Ebionites, Adoptionists, Patripassianists, and Quartodecimans.

Lampe, Peter, *From Paul to Valentinus: Christians at Rome in the First Two Centuries* **(Minneapolis: Fortress Press, 2003).** This book may be the most important sociological and historical study ever written on Christianity in Rome. Professor Lampe uses data from archaeology, history, theology, and sociology to provide a comprehensive study of the rise of Christianity and its formation in Rome out of the Jewish community there. He investigates the literature associated with the Roman Christian community, including Paul's letter to the Romans and the writings of Clement of Rome, Justin Martyr, Montanus, and Valentinus.

Lüdemann, Gerd, *Heretics: The Other Side of Early Christianity* **(Louisville, Ky.: Westminster John Knox Press, 1996).** Professor Lüdemann offers a scholarly look at how the original form of Jewish Christianity became a second-century heresy. Also included is a major discussion of Paul and his legacy among the heretics, including the emergence of Marcion. The Johannine letters are discussed as representative of their own form of heresy. He traces the origins of the Apostles' Creed and the New Testament canon.

Marjanen, Antti and Luomanen, Petri (eds.), *A Companion to Second-Century Christian 'Heretics'*, **Supplements to Vigiliae Christianae 76 (Leiden: E. J. Brill, 2005).** This volume contains up-to-date academic essays from a number of scholars on the various forms of Christianity embraced by their followers as legitimate, but which have been largely

forgotten. Includes chapters on Basilides (by Birger Pearson), Sethian-
ism (by Michael Williams), the Valentinians (by Ismo Dunderberg),
Marcion (by Heikki Räisänen), Tatian (by William Petersen),
Bardaisan (by Nicola Denzey), Montanism (by Antti Marjanen),
Cerinthus (by Matti Myllykoski), the Ebionites (by Sakari Häkkinen),
the Nazarenes (by Petri Luomanen), Jewish Christianity (by F. Stanley
Jones), and the Elchasaites (by Gerard P. Luttikhuizen).

Staniforth, Maxwell and Louth, Andrew, *Early Christian Writings* **(New
York: Viking Penguin, 1st edn. 1968, 2nd edn. 1987).** An edited collection
of the Apostolic Fathers, including writings of Clement of Rome,
Ignatius of Antioch, and Polycarp of Smyrna, as well as the *Letter of
Diognetus*, **the** *Letter of Barnabas*, and the *Didache*. Each piece is
introduced by Andrew Louth.

The New Testament Apocrypha

Cameron, Ron, *The Other Gospels: Non-Canonical Gospel Texts* **(Philadelphia: Westminster Press, 1982).** This is an anthology of Gospel
literature, not from the New Testament, but from the Apocrypha and
Nag Hammadi literature. Sixteen texts are collected in English
translation, with substantial introductions by Professor Cameron. He
stresses the importance of these texts for our understanding of the Bible
and early Christianity.

J. K. Elliott (ed.), *The Apocryphal New Testament: A Collection of
Apocryphal Christian Literature in an English Translation Based on M.
R. James* **(Oxford: Clarendon Press, 1993).** These English translations of
the New Testament Apocrypha are based on an edition of this book
published by M. R. James in 1924. Dr. Elliott presents new translations
with short introductions and a more recent bibliography for those who
wish to pursue further study. This collection gives English readers
complete access to the Christian Apocrypha, with a few samples of
some Gnostic texts from Nag Hammadi.

Evans, Craig A., *Ancient Texts for New Testament Studies: A Guide to the
Background Literature* **(Peabody, Mass.: Hendrickson Publishers, 2005).**
This book surveys all the non-canonical literature of relevance to the
study of the New Testament and early Christianity. Summaries of
hundreds of documents are included, as well as notes about where the
original-language versions and English translations can be found and
bibliographies for further consultation. Huge appendices complete the

book, covering parallels in the New Testament and the apocryphal Gospels, parables and miracle stories associated with Jesus and other rabbis, canons of scripture, and messianic claimants.

Hennecke, Edgar and Schneemelcher, Wilhelm, *New Testament Apocrypha,* **2 vols. (Philadelphia: Westminster Press, 1963).** This is the classic two-volume set, covering the importance of the apocryphal texts. Volume 1 includes the apocryphal Gospels, while vol. 2 has writings related to the apostles, apocalypses, and related subjects. Translations and standard (albeit older) introductions to each text comprise this important academic contribution.

Klauck, Hans-Josef, *Apocryphal Gospels: An Introduction* **(London: T&T Clark, 2003).** This is a fairly comprehensive though brief introduction to the apocryphal Gospels. Each text is classified under a heading, including Jewish-Christian Gospels, infancy Gospels, death and resurrection Gospels, Nag Hammadi Gospels, dialogue Gospels, and legends. Each section has an up-to-date bibliography for those seeking additional resources.

Koester, Helmut, *Ancient Christian Gospels: Their History and Development* **(Philadelphia: Trinity Press International, 1990).** This is a standard text for the study of early Christian Gospels. It progresses chronologically, with Professor Koester giving scholarly analyses of each Gospel, canonical or otherwise. He covers the earliest collections of Jesus' sayings, including Q and the *Gospel of Thomas,* as well as the canonical Gospels, the *Gospel of Peter,* and the sayings tradition embedded in the writings of the Church Fathers.

Lapham, Fred, *An Introduction to the New Testament Apocrypha* **(London: T&T Clark, 2003).** An introduction to the literature written by Christians in the second and third centuries which we collectively know as the New Testament Apocrypha. It is valuable in that it arranges the materials as indigenous Christian literature in various geographical locales, including the Judaean church, the church in Samaria, the church in Syria, the church in Mesopotamia, the churches of Asia, and the church in Egypt. The brief surveys of each piece of literature are academic yet readable.

Moreschini, Claudio and Norelli, Enrico, *Early Christian Greek and Latin Literature: A Literary History,* **vol. 1 (Peabody, Mass.: Hendrickson Publishers, 2005).** Provides substantial surveys of literature from Paul to the age of Constantine, the ante-Nicene period. What is particularly provocative and refreshing about this volume is that it makes no distinction between canonical and non-canonical literature, so the reader gets a real sense of the diversity of thought in early Christianity. Coverage is quite thorough, including the New Testament, extra-canonical Gospels, Gnosticism, Montanism, the Greek Apologists, the literature of the martyrs, early Christian poetry, and the Church Fathers.

Gnosis and the Gnostics

Barnstone, Willis and Meyer, Marvin (eds.), *The Gnostic Bible. Gnostic Texts of Mystical Wisdom from the Ancient and Medieval Worlds: Pagan, Jewish, Christian, Mandaean, Manichaean, Islamic, and Cathar* **(Boston: Shambhala, 2003).** This is a wonderful collection because of its breadth: a volume that contains literature from so many sources, including Gnostic texts like the *Book of Baruch*, Sethian literature, Valentinian texts, Thomasine material, and even the *Naassene Sermon*. But that is not all. The anthology also contains Hermetic, Mandaean, Manichaean, Islamic, and Cathar literature. All the original texts are in English translation with readable and accessible introductions by scholars. Bear in mind that the book is a selection of texts from antiquity. It does not contain every known Gnostic text.

Couliano, Ioan P., *The Tree of Gnosis: Gnostic Mythology from Early Christianity to Modern Nihilism* **(San Francisco: Harper, 1992).** This is a work influenced by the comparative perspective of Mircea Eliade. Professor Couliano focuses on the Gnostic (and perennial) view that understands reality in terms of separate and radically opposing absolutes, as a division between God and creation, between good and evil, between the spiritual and the material. He takes the reader through a myriad of traditions including Marcionism, Manichaeism, Paulician-ism, Bogomilism, the Cathars, and modern Nihilism.

Filoramo, Giovanni, *A History of Gnosticism* **(Oxford: Blackwell, 1990).** Professor Filoramo thinks that Gnosticism originated in the second century as an alternative religion to Christianity and paganism. Central to Gnosticism is the belief that the body and its passions are evil. Gnosis is the secret revelation known to Gnostic initiates which allowed them to transcend their bodies and the cosmic realm to achieve spiritual resurrection. His book is arranged topically rather than chronologically.

Foerster, Werner, *Gnosis: A Selection of Gnostic Texts,* **2 vols. (Oxford: Clarendon Press, 1972, 1974).** These two volumes are an anthology of references to *Gnosis* from the Church Fathers (vol. 1) and the Coptic and Mandaic literature (vol. 2). This is an indispensable set (albeit out of print) because it collates the original references from the Christian literature and arranges them in chapters devoted to each Gnostic thinker or Gnostic group.

Jonas, Hans, *The Gnostic Religion: The Message of the Alien God and the Beginnings of Christianity*, **3rd edn. (Boston: Beacon Press, 2001).** Actually a revision of a classic originally published in 1953. Whenever I ask my students to read this book, I tell them that although it is out of date, Professor Jonas captures the spirit of Gnosis. As his title indicates, he understands Gnosticism to have been a religious movement in antiquity with its main tenets, imagery, and symbolic language all closely associated with the Greek world of ideas. He covers several systems of Gnostic thought including Simon Magus, the Hymn of the Pearl, Marcion, Hermetism, Valentinianism, and Manichaeism.

King, Karen L., *Revelation of the Unknowable God, with Text, Translation, and Notes to NHC XI,3 Allogenes* **(Sonoma, Calif.: Polebridge Press, 1995).** This book is excellent, in that it contains not only a new translation of the Nag Hammadi text *Allogenes*, but also a substantial overview of Sethianism. It is very readable, with extensive notes.

King, Karen L., *The Secret Revelation of John* **(Cambridge, Mass.: Harvard University Press, 2006).** This is Professor King's reading of the *Apocryphon of John* beyond the academic category of "Gnosticism." She shows how the Jewish scripture was read by some early Christians in radical ways as revisions of the traditional interpretations. A new translation of the *Apocryphon of John* is included.

King, Karen L., *What is Gnosticism?* **(Cambridge, Mass.: Harvard University Press, 2003).** Professor King writes about how historians have been misled about Christianity in the second century by the polemical writings of the Church Fathers, which characterize certain Christians as Gnostics and heretics. This characterization is a reflection of the battle over orthodoxy, rather than a historical reality. Because of this, she wishes to disentangle modern historiography from the early Christian voices, and to abandon the word "Gnosticism."

Layton, Bentley, *The Gnostic Scriptures: A New Translation with Annotations and Introductions by Bentley Layton* **(New York: Doubleday, 1987).** This book is designed for the general reader, although I would not characterize it as "introductory." Professor Layton provides fresh English translations of much of the Gnostic literature and provides valuable introductions to each text and each Gnostic school, as he prefers to call them. He covers the classic Gnostic texts, the writings of Valentinus and his school, the school of Thomas, and other early currents in Gnosticism.

Logan, Alastair, *The Gnostics: Identifying an Early Christian Cult* **(London: T&T Clark, 2006).** This book explores the existence of a Gnostic cult movement in antiquity, one that has a particular theology, liturgy, and practice. Dr. Logan thinks that this cult movement originated in the late first century and arose out of Christianity. In his book, he examines the self-identity of the Gnostics over and against those he calls the catholics. He seeks to reconstruct the Gnostic initiation ritual from the Nag Hammadi texts. He thinks that the early third-century Hypogeum of Aurelii in Rome was a cult centre for the Gnostics.

Markschies, Christoph, *Gnosis: An Introduction* **(London: T&T Clark, 2003).** Professor Markschies provides us with a succinct new introduction to Gnosis in antiquity. He understands Gnosis to be a set of beliefs from which emerged a distinct movement within the Christian church. His book covers briefly the early forms of Gnosis, as well as later representatives like Valentinus, Marcion, and Mani.

Meyer, Marvin, *The Gnostic Discoveries: The Impact of the Nag Hammadi Library* **(San Francisco: Harper, 2005).** Professor Meyer's book is an accessible introduction to the literature found in the Nag Hammadi collection. He tells us about the discovery of the Nag Hammadi library, the meaning of the collection as a whole, the wisdom of the Thomasine texts, the meaning of the Sethian materials, the view of salvation found in the Valentinian texts, and what we can know (or perhaps cannot know) about several ambiguous Gnostic documents.

Pagels, Elaine, *The Gnostic Gospels* **(New York: Vintage Books, 1979).** One of the classic books on Gnosis in ancient Christianity. Professor Pagels examines the different ways that orthodox Christians and Gnostics thought about God, Christ, and the church. She asks whose version of Christianity won and why, suggesting that the reasons were more than theological musings: they were political and social rather than religious. In more recent books, Professor Pagels has argued that the category of Gnosticism should be abandoned, and appears to prefer to no longer use it.

Pearson, Birger, *Ancient Gnosticism: Traditions and Literature* **(Minneapolis: Fortress Press, 2007).** This is the most recent and up-to-date introduction to Gnosis. Professor Pearson has written an accessible introduction that is well aware of the scholarly debates in the field. He understands Gnosticism as a useful category within the Graeco-Roman religious world. He proceeds historically, writing about the earliest Gnostic teachers, Sethian or Classic Gnosticism, the Gnostic Gospels, Basilides, Valentinus, Gnostic systems of Three Principles, Gnostic writings of uncertain affiliation, Hermetic Gnosis, Manichaeism, and Mandaeanism.

Pétrement, Simone, *A Separate God: The Christian Origins of Gnosticism* (San Francisco: Harper, 1984). Professor Pétrement does not think that Gnosticism is a pre-Christian system of beliefs, but believes it only emerged out of Christianity to be suppressed later by the orthodox Church Fathers as heresy. In this book, she advances this theory by examining the principal Gnostic doctrines including theological dualism, the seven creator angels, God the Mother, God the Man, the role of a redeemer, docetism, and salvation through Gnosis. All of these doctrines, she claims, originated from interpretations of Paul and John.

Robinson, James M. (general ed.), *The Nag Hammadi Library in English*, 4th edn. (Leiden: E. J. Brill, 1996). This is the complete collection of all the Nag Hammadi texts in English translation, and also the *Gospel of Mary*. It includes a substantial introduction by Professor Robinson about the Nag Hammadi discovery. Each translation begins with a brief introduction to the text by a scholar.

Roukema, Riemer, *Gnosis and Faith in Early Christianity* (Harrisburg, Pa.: Trinity Press International, 1999). A basic introduction to Gnosticism as it emerges in early Christianity. Dr. Roukema provides background information on Gnosticism within ancient philosophy, Judaism, and the mystery religions. He understands Gnosticism to be a Hellenized form of Christianity.

Rudolph, Kurt, *Gnosis: The Nature and History of Gnosticism* (San Francisco: Harper, 1983). This is the only "textbook" on Gnosticism of which I am aware. It is a standard work, dealing quite well with historical issues. Professor Rudolph provides a comprehensive analysis, liberally supplying quotations from the Nag Hammadi sources and the writings of the Church Fathers. He divides his book into several sections, including a long discussion of the sources for the study of Gnosis, the nature and structure of Gnostic ideology and mythology, and the history of Gnosis through the Mandaeans.

Thomassen, Einar, *The Spiritual Seed: The Church of the 'Valentinians'*, Nag Hammadi and Manichaean Studies 60 (Leiden: E. J. Brill). Professor Thomassen provides us with a comprehensive historical look at the Valentinians from the beginning of the movement to its later forms, including discussions of the differences between the eastern and

western branches of Valentinianism. Also featured are discussions of
Valentinian theology (ideas about the incarnation, the beginnings of the
cosmos, salvation) and practice (initiation rituals).

Turner, John D., *Sethian Gnosticism and the Platonic Tradition* **(Québec
City: University of Laval, 2001).** This is *the* book on Sethianism. It is
comprehensive and academic, but still readable. Not an aspect is missed
in this volume, which covers Sethian Gnosticism and Platonism in the
first five centuries. Professor Turner's analysis is systematic and
detailed, so be ready with the Nag Hammadi collection at hand while
reading it.

Williams, Michael Allen, *Rethinking "Gnosticism": An Argument for
Dismantling a Dubious Category* **(Princeton: Princeton University Press,
1996).** Professor Williams argues convincingly that the term "Gnosticism" gives the false impression that there existed in antiquity a single
religious movement that opposed the prevailing religions in the ancient
world. He shows that "Gnosticism" is a modern construct that does not
adequately describe the ancient people who identified themselves as
Gnostics. These people and their beliefs were diverse, and do not allow
us to lump them easily into particular categories on the basis of their
views on the body, the cosmos, and salvation.

A Synopsis of Sethian Gnostic Literature

Title and Probable date	Content
Sophia of Jesus Christ Late 1st or early 2nd c.	Nag Hammadi Codex III, 4; Berlin Gnostic Codex 8502, 3; Papyrus Oxyrhynchus 1081. This text is a Gnostic revision of a famous older philosophical tract. It is recast as a revelation dialogue between Jesus and some of his disciples, including Philip, Matthew, Thomas, Bartholomew, and Mary. The markers in the text, including Sophia, Autogenes, and Ialdabaoth, suggest Sethian influence. It does not appear, however, to contain the developed Sethian mythology that we find in later Sethian texts. So some scholars have understood this text in terms of "proto-Sethianism."
Apocryphon of John Early 2nd c.	Nag Hammadi Codex II, 1; III, 1; IV, 1; Berlin Gnostic Papyri 8502, 2. Perhaps the most widespread and well-known Gnostic text in antiquity. Four copies have survived in addition to Bishop Irenaeus' report in *Against Heresies* 1.29–30, which appears dependent on an early version of this text. The *Apocryphon* contains a thorough telling of the entire Sethian myth. This myth has been recast within a Christian dialogue between the post-resurrection Jesus and John the son of Zebedee.
Trimorphic Protennoia Early 2nd c.	Nag Hammadi Codex XIII, 1. Another old Sethian text, perhaps contemporaneous with the *Apocryphon of John*. Its name means the Triple-Formed First Thought of God. It describes three descents of First

Thought or Protennoia, the last of these being framed as an exegesis on the prologue of the Gospel of John. This text contains some very old Sethian poetry, perhaps sung as hymns, that pre-date the writing of the text itself. The poetry is in the form of aretalogies, which are first-person recitations. When Protennoia descends the third time as the Logos and assumes human form, it reveals to us the rite of the five seals, a baptismal ceremony that liberates the soul.

Apocalypse of Adam
Mid-2nd c.

Nag Hammadi Codex V, 5. This text is written as a revelation delivered to Adam, which he, in turn, tells to his son Seth. The text contains no explicit reference to Christianity except for the last line, which contains a name that appears to be a form of Jesus of Nazareth (Yesseus Mazareus). Thus this text has been used as evidence for the existence of a Jewish form of Gnosticism that may have pre-dated its Christian incarnation. The content focuses on how Adam and Eve came to lose Gnosis, with the consequence that their lifespan was shortened. The *Apocalypse of Adam* contains a poem about the thirteen Kingdoms of the universe and a redeemer figure who appears to be traveling through them. The remainder of the revelation centers on how Seth and his offspring will be preserved and carry on Gnosis despite the flood and conflagration sent by Ialdabaoth. The text ends with the revelation of the hidden Gnosis in terms of a rite of holy baptism known to Seth and passed on to his descendants.

Hypostasis of
the Archons
Mid-2nd c.

Nag Hammadi Codex II, 4. Also called the *Reality of the Rulers*. This tract is a Gnostic midrash on Genesis 1–6. It contains Christian features, but these are not dominant. In fact, they function to open the work, with a reference to Colossians and Ephesians. This introduction could easily have been added to an older Jewish Gnostic interpretation of the Genesis story. There is some kind of literary connection between this text and *On the Origin of the World*, most likely a common earlier source that both texts rely on. The content focuses on the deeds of the Archons as they create and enslave Adam and Eve. The birth of their four children, Cain, Abel, Seth and Norea, is recounted. The tract includes a long Gnostic revelation to Norea from the great angel Eleleth.

Thought of Norea
Mid-2nd c.

Nag Hammadi Codex IX, 2. This text is very short, only 52 lines. Because it is a hymn, this text is also known as the *Ode on Norea*. It is very balanced in terms of structure, reflecting Hebrew poetry with its emphasis on the repetition of parallels. It is not metered according to the tastes of Greek poetry, which suggests a Jewish origin. The hymn has four parts: an invocation to the Father, Mother, and Son; an invocation to Norea; Norea's teaching; and Norea's redemption with the intercession of Harmozel, Oroiael, Daveithe, and Eleleth. No Christian elements are present.

Gospel of Judas
Mid-2nd c.

Tchacos Codex. This text is thoroughly Christian, yet contains a ratcheting polemic against apostolic Christianity. It purports to be a narrative of Jesus' teachings and interpretations of dreams, delivered to the twelve disciples and Judas during the eight-day celebration of Passover, three days before the Passover meal. Judas is identified with the Thirteenth Demon, Ialdabaoth-Nebruel. As a demon, Judas recognizes Jesus while the other disciples do not, a feature this Gospel derived from the Gospel of Mark. Jesus reveals to Judas his awful fate and his connection to the Archons, and his future destruction at the end of time. Judas resists and, out of wrath, betrays Jesus. The text is very critical of the doctrine of apostolic succession, the interpretation of Jesus' death as a vicarious atonement, and the efficacy of the eucharist. It also contains a substantial narration of the Sethian myth, particularly the creation of the third Aeon, Autogenes, where the Gnostic generation resides, and the creation and rule of this universe by the Archons.

Holy Book of the Great Invisible Spirit or *Gospel of the Egyptians*
Mid- to late 2nd c.

Nag Hammadi Codex III, 2; IV, 2. We have two Coptic manuscripts of this work, which differ substantially from each other. The *Holy Book* is claimed to have been written by Seth and hidden on a mountain. It contains a version of the Sethian myth, much of it written in high liturgical style. It contains old hymns and chants that were used in worship and contemplation. The first part narrates the origin of the Pleromic world. The second part describes the offspring of Seth, whom the Archons try to destroy, and their preservation. Seth descends as Jesus and saves his children. It concludes with a section that acknowledges the authorship and secrecy of the text. This tract contains a generous number of references to the five seals and baptism. It is a thoroughly Christian composition.

Thunder: Perfect Mind
Mid- to late 2nd c.

Nag Hammadi Codex VI, 2. This is a poem or hymn written in the first person from the perspective of a female Aeon, called "Perfect Intellect," an epithet for Barbelo. So it may be a Sethian composition. It weaves together "I am" declarations with exhortations and reproaches to the listeners. The speaker is sent to humans from "the power" above. She summons those who will listen to her. Those who respond will be liberated. This hymn has connections with hymns about Eve in *On the Origin of the World* and the *Hypostasis of the Archons*. So its opposing images appear to be a riddle whose answer is "Eve," a point first made by Professor Bentley Layton.

Melchizedek
Late 2nd c.

Nag Hammadi Codex IX, 1. The features of this text suggest that it is an apocalypse. It is a revelation granted to the high priest Melchizedek (Genesis 14.18; Psalm 110.4). Although fragmentary, it contains vivid liturgical fragments, prayers, and hymns, indicative of a cultic document. It opens with a dialogue between Jesus Christ and Melchizedek, but turns into a revelation given by Gamaliel, one of the angels of the Luminaries of Autogenes. It is a thoroughly Christian document, predicting Jesus' ministry, death, and resurrection. Melchizedek undertakes an initiation that includes a thanksgiving prayer, baptism, the reception of a priestly name, and performance of a spiritual offering. More revelation shows Melchizedek that he will be Jesus crucified and resurrected, the one who will triumph over the Archons.

Second Treatise of the Great Seth
Early 3rd c.

Nag Hammadi Codex VII, 2. Some scholars do not consider this text Sethian because Seth is not mentioned in the body of the tractate. However, this Gnostic text contains many of the mythic characters associated with the Sethian myth, including Sophia, Ialdabaoth, Adonaios, and Ennoia. So in my opinion its connection to Sethianism is almost certain. It is a completely Christian text, with the focus on the descent of the Christ into Jesus, his crucifixion, and his victory over the Archons. The crucifixion scene is similar to what we know about Basilides' teaching on the subject, and suggests a sharing of knowledge between the Sethian and Basilidian Christians.

Zostrianos
Early 3rd c.

Nag Hammadi Codex VIII, 1. An apocalypse that includes a heavenly journey, with Zostrianos as the one who ascends. He may be the same as the famous character in antiquity known as the magus Zoroaster of Persia. The ascent takes place as a result of a number of baptisms that Zostranios performs in the various realms and Aeons. Liturgies, hymns, and prayers are strewn throughout the text, giving us a good amount of information about ritual practices. Large sections of the text are damaged, so much of the original work is lost. The ideas in the text represent a Platonic interpretation of classic Sethian mythology. In fact, this is probably a version of the text mentioned by Porphyry as an apocalypse in use in Plotinus' day (*Life of Plotinus* 16).

Allogenes
Early 3rd c.

Nag Hammadi Codex XI, 3. This apocalypse has as its central figure Allogenes the Foreigner. He is the recipient of visions which he records for Messos, his son. Allogenes shows how to overcome fear and ignorance, to contemplate every level of the Gnostic journey, and to ascend to the highest Aeon possible, attaining to the primary revelation of the Unknown God. Hymns, prayers, chants, and references to some ritual activity are present. This text interprets the Sethian mythology in terms of Platonism. It is probably a version of a text mentioned in Porphyry, when it is said that Plotinus taught a course "Against the Gnostics" who wrote "revelations by Zoroaster and Zostrianos and Nicotheos and Allogenes and Messos and other such people (*Life of Plotinus* 16)."

Fragment of Allogenes and Satan
Early 3rd c.

Tchacos Codex. Fragment of a text featuring the redeemer Allogenes. In the extant portion, Allogenes encounters Satan at Mount Tabor. He is tempted and overcomes Satan through personal prayer. The story is written in the first person from the perspective of Allogenes.

Three Steles of Seth
Early 3rd c.

Nag Hammadi Codex VII, 5. This is an amazing text, amazing text, because it is a liturgical handbook containing the actual prayers, hymns, and chants used to initiate the journey of the spirit into the upper three Aeons. So the first part of the text is the liturgy devoted to the Aeon Autogenes, the second to the Aeon Barbelo, and the third to the Father. The ascent was probably believed to occur in this order. Neo-Platonic terminology abounds, suggesting that this text is connected with other Platonized Sethian treatises.

Marsanes
Late 3rd c.

Nag Hammadi Codex X, 1. The name attributed to this text was known to have belonged to a Gnostic prophet and visionary, according to the *Untitled Treatise* in the Bruce Codex. Epiphanius also refers to him in his writings against heresies (40.7.6). This document purports to be the visions and revelations of this prophet. There are numerous references to ritual practices, prayers, and chants, including baptism. There appear to be thirteen seals, marking each level of ascent through the realms and Aeons. Like the other Sethian texts produced in the third century, it is heavily Platonized. There is some evidence that it may be contemporaneous with Iamblichus.

Untitled
Treatise
Late 3rd c. or
early 4th c.

Bruce Codex. This text is similar to the *Holy Book of Book of the Great Invisible Spirit* and *Zostrianos*. But there is evidence for some type of dependence on *Marsanes* or knowledge of this document. It contains a detailed Sethian mythology. Christ reveals, through Setheus, the baptismal rite needed for initiation into the Aeons. It is completely Platonized.

Testimony from the Church Fathers on the *Gospel of Judas*

Bishop Irenaeus of Lyons, *Against Heresies* 1.31.1. Late second century.

"Other [Gnostics] declare that Cain derived his being from the Power above, and acknowledge that Esau, Korah, the Sodomites, and all such persons, are related to themselves. On this account, they add, they have been assailed by the Creator, yet none of them has suffered injury. For Sophia was in the habit of carrying off that which belonged to her from them to herself. They declare that Judas the traitor was thoroughly acquainted with these things, and that he alone, knowing the truth as none of the others did, accomplished the mystery of the betrayal. By him all things, both earthly and heavenly, were thus thrown into confusion. They produce a fictitious history of this kind, which they entitle the Gospel of Judas."

Commentary

Irenaeus' scathing treatise is the first to mention the *Gospel of Judas* and its contents. In this passage, he does not give us much detail, but suggests only that the *Gospel of Judas* had Judas as the central figure, that Judas was taught the "truth" while the other disciples were not, and that his betrayal of Jesus was a mystery that set the earth and heavens into chaos. He never says that Judas was characterized as "good" or a "hero" in the *Gospel of Judas*. It is difficult to know from his description whether he actually read a version of the *Gospel of Judas* we possess, or was simply testifying to hearsay about its contents, or worst of all, was guessing at them. I tend to think that his description is a highly accurate account of the manuscript we possess, except that he identifies it as a Gospel belonging to people who declared that their ancestors were Cain, Esau, Korah, and the Sodomites. Since the people who wrote the *Gospel of Judas* understood themselves to be descendants of the great Seth, not Cain or any of the others whom Irenaeus names, this suggests to me that his genealogy is fictitious, serving only to undermine the Gospel's credibility. It is interesting, however, that the Sethians taught that Cain was a Power. In the Sethian system, however, he was not a benevolent Power, but an evil Archon. So if the Sethians taught that the human Cain owed his existence to a Power above, he owed it to an evil one, not a good one.

Pseudo-Tertullian, *Against All Heresies* 2.5–6. Early third century, falsely attributed to Tertullian of Carthage.

"There has broken out another heresy also, which is called that of the Cainites. And the reason for this is that they magnify Cain as if he had been conceived of some potent virtue which operated in him. For Abel had procreated after being conceived of an inferior virtue, and accordingly had been found inferior. They who assert this likewise defend the traitor Judas, telling us that he is admirable and great, because of the advantages he is vaunted to have conferred on humankind. For some [of them] think that gratitude is to be given to Judas on this account, that is, they say, 'When Judas observed that Christ wanted to subvert the truth, he betrayed him so that there would not be any possibility that the truth would be subverted.' And other people argue against them, and say, 'Because the powers of this world were unwilling that Christ should suffer, lest through his death salvation should be prepared for humankind, he, consulting for the salvation of humankind, betrayed Christ, so that there might not be any possibility at all for salvation to be impeded, which was being impeded through the virtues that were opposing Christ's passion. And thus, through the passion of Christ, there might not be any possibility of the salvation of humankind being delayed."

Commentary

Pseudo-Tertullian suggests that there was a Gnostic group who called themselves the Cainites, believing Cain to be a superior being of some great virtue. They defend Judas' actions, even thinking them admirable because he helped to save humanity. Some Cainites speculated that Jesus baulked at his mission, so that Judas was instrumental in ensuring that the truth was not subverted. Others thought that the Archons or rulers of this world did not want Jesus to be crucified because they knew that this would bring about salvation, freeing humanity from their grip. So Judas stepped in as the supreme God's agent, carrying out God's plan for redemption through the cross. Notice that Pseudo-Tertullian makes no mention of the *Gospel of Judas* and his remarks show no familiarity with the text we possess. Not only does the text identify itself with the Gnostics descended from Seth, never mentioning Cain, but it also does not allude to any desire by Jesus to subvert the truth or the Archons' wish to prevent the crucifixion because the supreme God planned to use it as a vehicle for redemption. In fact, our Gospel states the opposite – that if Judas is a demon working for the Archons and he brought about Jesus' sacrifice, then the sacrifice he made was not to the supreme God, but to the demons who rule this world.

Bishop Epiphanius of Salamis, *The Medicine Chest* 38.1.2–5; 38.3.1–5. Late fourth century.

"They say that Cain is from the stronger power and the dominion from above, as are also Esau, the company of Korah, and the Sodomites, while Abel is of the weaker power. All of them are praiseworthy and their kin. They boast of being related to Cain, the Sodomites, Esau, and Korah. These, they say, are of the perfect knowledge from above. For this reason, they say, although the maker of this world devoted himself to their annihilation, he could in no way harm them, for they were hidden from him and transported to the upper Aeon whence the stronger power is. Sophia let them approach her, for they belonged to her. For this reason they say that Judas knew quite well all about these matters. They consider him their kinsman and count him among those possessing the highest knowledge, so that they also carry around a short writing in his name which they call the Gospel of Judas ...

"These fables they mix in with the mischievous ignorance they teach, advising their disciples that every person must choose for himself the stronger power and separate himself from the inferior and feebler, namely the one which made heaven, the flesh, and the world, and pass above to the highest regions through Christ's crucifixion. For it was for this reason, they say, that he came from above, that a strong power might be made active in him which would triumph over the weaker power and hand over the body. Now some of them teach this, but others say something else. Some of them say that it was because Christ was wicked that he was betrayed by Judas, because he, Christ, wanted to distort what pertains to the law. They admire Cain and Judas, as I said, and they say, 'For this reason he betrayed him, because he wanted to destroy sound teachings.' But others among them say, 'Not at all. He betrayed him, although he was good, because of his [Judas'] knowledge of heavenly things. For', they say, 'the Archons knew that if Christ were given over to the cross, their feeble power would be drained. Judas, knowing this, bent every effort to betray him, thereby accomplishing a good work for salvation. We should admire and praise him, because through him the salvation of the cross was prepared for us and the revelation of things above occasioned by it.'"

Commentary

Bishop Epiphanius is writing about a heretical group he calls "Cainites." He mentions that they have the *Gospel of Judas*, which tells the story of Judas their ancestor. Judas had higher knowledge and should be commended because, without him, salvation would not have been achieved. Like Pseudo-Tertullian, Epiphanius does not know the *Gospel of Judas* we possess, but appears to be passing along a story that had been fabricated long before him about a fictitious group of Gnostic Christians called the Cainites. This invention was likely the result of (mis)reading Irenaeus.

APPENDIX 4

Q&A with April DeConick

Can you tell me a little about the background of the Gospel of Judas? When does it date from, where was it found?

The manuscript was discovered in the 1970s in an ancient catacomb that was being looted by local peasants living near the cliffs of the Jebel Qarara. The Jebel Qarara hills are only a few minutes on foot from the Nile River not far from El Minya, Egypt. Although we know that the Gospel of Judas existed in the middle of the second century because Bishop Irenaeus of Lyons mentions it (ca. 180), the manuscript that we have is a fourth- or fifth-century Coptic translation. It was only one text in a book of Gnostic Christian writings.

It was buried along with three other books that had been copied in the fourth or fifth centuries – a book of Paul's letters in Coptic, the book of Exodus in Greek, and a mathematical treatise in Greek. All four books had been sealed in a white limestone box and buried in a family tomb. If nothing else, their burial in this tomb points to their favoritism in the life of an early Christian living in ancient Egypt, a Christian who seems to have had esoteric leanings, and no difficulty studying canonical favorites alongside the Gnostic Gospel of Judas. In fact, he appears to have wanted to take them with him in death.

Why did it take so long to make the first English translation?

The English translation wasn't what took so long. What took the time was recovering the text from the antiquities market, which finally was done in the early 2000s. It also took time to restore the manuscript so that it could be read. The book that contains the Gospel of Judas was in the worst possible shape due to terrible handling once it left the grave. It had been torn in parts to make quicker and more profitable sales. The pages had been reshuffled so that the original pagination was gone. It was brittle and crumbling thanks to a stay in someone's freezer. The ink was barely legible because of exposure to the elements. Members of the National Geographic team have told me that initially they photocopied every fragment and then used the photocopies to piece together the pages. They worked with tweezers to fit together the shards of papyrus and also relied on state-of-the-art computer technology.

Once the restoration was complete, the manuscript could be read. It is written in an old Egyptian language called Coptic. The Coptic text had to be transcribed, which was no small job given the fragmented nature of the restored pages and the eroded ink. After the initial transcription was made, it was then translated into English.

What was it about the National Geographic translation that inspired you to make your own translation?

When National Geographic finally released the transcription and translation of the Gospel of Judas, I was enthusiastic because my area of expertise is ancient Gnostic religiosity and early Christian mysticism. Most of my career as a professor has been devoted to the study of the Nag Hammadi texts.

The Gospel of Judas came upon most of us out of a whirlwind. I had heard whispers about the Gospel of Judas for years, but nothing really concrete. Then there it was captured on film and on the web. I was repelled by the sensationalism of its release, but still attracted to the idea that here was a brand new Gnostic text that no one has read for *how many centuries*?! I guess I wanted to know what stories it had to tell us about the Christians who wrote it in the second century. And once I started to work out my own translation, I realized that I had an obligation to other scholars and to the public to set the record straight about what the Gospel of Judas actually says.

What makes your interpretation so different from the NG version?

For a long time, scholars have thought that the Gospel of Judas featured a Judas hero because testimony from a couple of Church Fathers led us to believe that there were a group of Gnostics known as Cainites. The Cainites were said to believe that all the bad characters in the Bible, including Judas, were actually heroes. I tend to be extremely skeptical of the testimony of the Church Fathers on these sorts of issues for the sheer fact that the Fathers saw the Gnostics as their opponents and they did everything they could to undermine them, including lying. So I didn't have an opinion on what the Gospel of Judas *should* say about Judas.

Once I started translating the Gospel of Judas and began to see the types of translation choices that the National Geographic team had made, I was startled and concerned. The text very clearly called Judas a "demon." Why did the team feel it necessary to translate this "spirit"? The text very clearly says that Judas will be "separated from" the Gnostics. Why did the team feel it necessary to translate this "set apart for" the Gnostics? And so forth.

I didn't care if Judas was good, bad or ugly. I just wanted to hear what the Sethian Gnostics had to say about him, and make sense of the text as a whole.

Why do you think that the NG interpretation doesn't work?

Not only is this interpretation based on a problematic English translation, rather than on what the Coptic actually says, but the opinion that Judas is a hero and a good guy is nonsense in terms of the bigger gospel narrative. For instance, this gospel berates sacrifice and understands it to be a horrifying practice dedicated to the god who wars against the supreme Father God. If this is the case, then Judas' sacrifice of Jesus simply cannot be a good thing. To say it is, is to rip apart the logic of what the text is saying as a whole.

Why do you think so many scholars and writers have been inspired by the NG version?

I have been truly amazed at the number of people who have jumped on this bandwagon. One of my colleagues upon hearing my concerns at a conference stood up and said, "I just don't see why Judas can't be good. We need a good Judas." This really stopped me in my tracks and took this discourse to an entirely new level for me.

There is something bigger going on here, in our modern communal psyche. I haven't been able to put my finger on it exactly, but it appears to have something to do with our collective guilt about anti-Semitism and our need to reform the relationship between Jews and Christians following World War II.

Judas has been a terrifying figure in our history, since he became in the Middle Ages the archetypal Jew who was responsible for Jesus' death. His story was abused for centuries as a justification to commit atrocities against Jews. I wonder if one of the ways that our communal psyche has handled this in recent decades is to try to erase or explain the evil Judas, to remove from him the guilt of Jesus' death. There are many examples of this in pop fiction and film produced after World War II. It seems to be that the National Geographic interpretation has grown out of this collective need and has been well-received because of it.

Why has no one challenged the NG version before now?

There have been challenges, but they are just now beginning to be published due to the year lag it takes to move something into press. Because the National Geographic team had exclusive rights for publication, the contents of the Gospel of Judas have been kept in strictest confidence and secrecy. The members of the team were required to sign non-disclosure statements in order to keep this secrecy until the Gospel was published in April 2006.

So the interpretation that this team spun is the only one that was allowed to emerge, and it did so as "the" authoritative interpretation. Scholars all over the world literally have been left behind by years because of this exclusivity. This has robbed the academic community of the opportunity to freely discuss this Gospel, offering different viewpoints, questioning transcriptional and translation choices, and so forth, *before* the release of a reliable critical edition.

What is worse is that National Geographic still has not released the photographs of the Gospel of Judas, so even the Coptic transcription they have provided us on the Web cannot be checked for accuracy. I hope that by the time this book is published, National Geographic will have released the critical edition with photographs, a project that was accomplished with little or no input from scholars beyond National Geographic's team.

Certainly National Geographic has had its exclusive, an exclusive that may have been very profitable for National Geographic, but it is a profit at the expense of our field, not only in terms of what the Gospel of Judas actually says, but also in terms of our reputation as professors and scholars.

Who do you think wrote the Gospel? Why do you think they wrote it?

The Gospel of Judas was written by Gnostic Christians called Sethians in the mid-second century. They wrote it to criticize Apostolic or mainstream Christianity, which they understood to be a form of Christianity that needed to reassess its faith. Particularly troubling for these Gnostic Christians was the Apostolic belief in the atonement, because this meant that God would have had to commit infanticide by sacrificing the Son.

They wrote the Gospel of Judas to prove that this could not be the case. Why? Because Judas was a demon who worked for another demon who rules this world and whose name is Ialdabaoth. How did they know this? Because Jesus had revealed this to Judas before Judas betrayed him. That is the bottom line. That is what this gospel says.

What do you think this manuscript tells us about early Christianity? Why is the Gospel of Judas important?

This gospel's voice is different. It represents the opinions of Christians in the second century who came to be labeled as "heretical" by later bishops who wished to gain control of the religious landscape. Because this is a Gnostic Christian tradition that did not survive, the chance find of this gospel has let us tune into a second century discussion about theology. And the voice we are hearing is the voice of the guy who lost the debate.

Not only is the recovery and integration of this voice into our history important, but also its contribution to Christian theology, which is enormous. The challenge against atonement theology as it is presented in the Gospel of Judas is a challenge that rocked the Apostolic Churches, forcing them to refine and recreate their position. The end result is a doctrine of atonement that became very popular in the Christian Church, a doctrine that understood the sacrifice of Jesus as a ransom paid to the Devil. This doctrine exists as a response to the Gnostic criticisms of atonement that we find in the Gospel of Judas.

What do you think it is about the figure of Judas that seems to fascinate both scholars and the general reader?

Judas Iscariot is a frightening figure. For Christians, he is the one who had it all, and yet betrayed God to his death for a few dollars. He is the archetype of human evil, the worst human being ever to live. He is the antithesis of the true Christian. Because of this, his image works as a religious control – he is someone the Christian never wants to become. For Jews, he is terrifying, the man whom Christians associated with Jewish people, whose story was used against them for centuries as a religious justification for their abuse and slaughter. Even his name "Judas" has been linked to "Jew," due to their root similarities (Judas/Judea/Jews). I think that Judas is someone whose shadow haunts us.

Notes

Preface

1 Madeleine Scopello (ed.), *L'Évangile de Judas: le contexte historique et littéraire d'un nouvel apocryphe/The Gospel of Judas: The Historical and Literary Context of a New Apocyphal Text* (Leiden: Brill, forthcoming).

Chapter 1: The Silenced Voice

1 Irenaeus, *Against Heresies* 1.31.1.

2 "The Gospel of Judas: The Lost Version of Christ's Betrayal," National Geographic Channel, First broadcast April 9, 2006.

3 The team responsible for the initial English translation consisted of Rodolphe Kasser, Gregor Wurst, Marvin Meyer, and François Gaudard. The commentary and interpretation is due to Rodolphe Kasser, Gregor Wurst, Marvin Meyer, and Bart Ehrman. I assume that the National Geographic publications represent mainly their opinions, and so it is to their collaborative work that I refer when using the phrase, "the team's translation and interpretation." This is not to say that other scholars were not also consulted by National Geographic (Stephen Emmel, Elaine Pagels, Donald Senior, and Craig A. Evans served as advisers) but I do not know the extent or tenor of their individual contributions. Craig A. Evans, however, appears to have largely agreed with the team's translation and interpretation when he wrote his appendix to his recent book, *Fabricating Jesus: How Modern Scholars Distort the Gospels* (Downers Grove, Ill.: Intervarsity Press, 2006), 240–5. This also appears to be the interpretative trajectory taken by Elaine Pagels in her new book co-authored with Karen King, *Reading Judas: The Gospel of Judas and the Shaping of Christianity* (New York: Viking, 2007).

4 All Coptic references in this book to the *Gospel of Judas* (except where noted otherwise) are taken from that web page, < http://www.nationalgeographic.com/lostgospel/document.html >. The Coptic transcription is a pdf file.

5 See Rodolphe Kasser, Marvin Meyer, and Gregor Wurst, with

additional commentary by Bart D. Ehrman, *The Gospel of Judas* (Washington, DC: National Geographic, 2006); "The Gospel of Judas: The Lost Version of Christ's Betrayal" Herbert Krosney, *The Lost Gospel of Judas: The Quest for the Gospel of Judas Iscariot* (Washington, DC: National Geographic, 2006). The transcription is established by Rodophe Kasser and Gregor Wurst, and will be referred to in this book as Kasser and Wurst, "Transcription."

6   Irenaeus, *Against Heresies* 1.10.1.
7   Ibid. 1.10.2–3.
8   1 Corinthians 15.3–5.
9   Justin Martyr, 1 *Apology* 26.
10 Tertullian, *Against Marcion* 5.19.
11 Cyril of Jerusalem, *Catechesis* 18.26.
12 Cited by Marco Frenschkowski, in Gerhard May and Katharina Greschat (eds), *Marcion and His Impact on Church History* (Berlin: Walter de Gruyter, 2002), 39–63.
13 Justin Martyr, *Dialogue with Trypho* 47.
14 Ibid.
15 John 14.16.
16 See John 16.13.
17 1 Corinthians 11.5; Acts 2.17–18; 21.8–10; cf. Acts 13.1.
18 Revelation 21.1–4, 10.
19 Revelation 14.3–5.
20 William Tabbernee, *Montanist Inscriptions and Testimonia: Epigraphic Sources Illustrating the History of Montanism,* North American Patristic Society Patristic Monograph Series 16 (Macon: Mercer University Press, 1997), 35–9.
21 Tertullian, *Against Praxeas* 1.
22 *Gospel of Philip* 52.21–25.
23 Clement of Alexandria, *Miscellanies* 1.145–1.146.4.

Chapter 2: A Gnostic Catechism

1   Irenaeus, *Against Heresies* 1.29–30.
2   Ibid.
3   Genesis 16.7–13.
4   Genesis 32.20; Exodus 33.20.
5   Exodus 3.1–6.
6   Genesis 3.8.
7   Deuteronomy 5.9.
8   Cf. Deuteronomy 6.15.
9   Isaiah 45.7.
10 Genesis 3.9.
11 Deuteronomy 32.39; Isaiah 43.10–11; 45.5–6, 18, 22; 46.9; 47.8, 10;

Hosea 13.4; Joel 2.27.
12 Baruch 3.29.
13 Wisdom of Ben Sirach 24.1–7; cf. Wisdom of Solomon 9.10.
14 Wisdom of Solomon 7.22–26.
15 Wisdom of Solomon 9.9; Wisdom of Ben Sirach 1.9; 24.9; Proverbs 8.22, 30.
16 Proverbs 3.18.
17 Proverbs 3.16; Wisdom of Solomon 7.27; 10.1–2.
18 Wisdom of Solomon 8.3–4.
19 *Apocryphon of John* 4.20–5.10.
20 *Gospel of Judas* 47.5–13.
21 *Gospel of Judas* 35.17–20.
22 *Gospel of Judas* 47.14–21.
23 *Gospel of Judas* 47.21–51.1.
24 *Gospel of Judas* 51.2–3.
25 *Apocryphon of John* 9.25–10.20. A number of meanings for this name have been proposed, including "begetter of Sabbaoth" and "Child of Chaos".
26 This relies on the Coptic reconstructin of the *Gospel of Judas* 52.5 made by John Turner, "The Place of the *Gospel of Judas* in Sethian Tradition," in Madeleine Scopello (ed.), *L'Évangile de Judas: le contexte historique et littéraire d'un nouvel apocryphe/The Gospel of Judas: The Historical and Literary Context of a New Apocryphal Text* (Leiden: Brill, forthcoming).
27 *Gospel of Judas* 51.4–52.14.
28 *Apocryphon of John* 29.23–25.
29 *Gospel of Judas* 52.15–55.21.
30 *Gospel of Judas* 54.8–13.

Chapter 3: A Mistaken Gospel

1   Rodolphe Kasser, Marvin Meyer, and Gregor Wurst, with additiónal commentary by Bart D. Ehrman, *The Gospel of Judas* (Washington, DC: National Geographic, 2006); "The Gospel of Judas: The Lost Version of Christ's Betrayal," National Geographic Channel, first broadcast April 9, 2006; Herbert Krosney, *The Lost Gospel: The Quest for the Gospel of Judas Iscariot* (Washington, DC: National Geographic, 2006). For more information about the National Geographic team, see Chapter 1, n. 3.
2   Kasser *et al.*, *The Gospel of Judas*, 129.
3   Ibid. 139; cf. 84, 97–101.
4   Ibid. 164–5.
5   Ibid. 101.
6   Ibid. 167.

7 See Chapter 1, n. 4.

8 Many of these same translation choices appear to have influenced Karen King in her translation of the *Gospel of Judas* in the book she wrote jointly with Elaine Pagels, *Reading Judas: The Gospel of Judas and the Shaping of Christianity* (New York: Viking, 2007). I will mention several of her translation choices in the notes.

9 *Gospel of Judas* 44.21.

10 Kasser *et al.*, *The Gospel of Judas*, 31. Karen King's translation gives a similar positive sense, supplying "god" as a translation of *daimon*: Pagels and King, *Reading Judas*, 115.

11 *Gospel of Judas* 35.7; 37.19; 43.19; 47.9; 49.12, 16; 53.17, 20, 23, 25; 54.5.

12 *Symposium* 202e–203a; Kasser *et al.*, *The Gospel of Judas*, p. 31 n. 74; cf. also pp. 163–6. Karen King justifies her translation of *daimon* as "god" with reference to Plato's *Phaedo* 83d-e.

13 Foerster, "δαιμων, δαιμόνιον, etc.," in Gerhard Kittel (ed.), Theological Dictionary of the New Testament (TNDT), vol. 2 (repr. Grand Rapids: Eerdmans, 1999), 2–3.

14 Ibid. 8.

15 Theodor Hopfner, *Griechisch-ägyptischer Offenbarungszauber*, vol. 1 (repr. Amsterdam: A. M. Hakkert, 1974), sec. 166.

16 Foerster, "δαιμων, δαιμόνιον, etc.," 5–6.

17 Ibid. 12–16.

18 Ibid. 16–20.

19 E. C. E. Owen, "Δαίμων and Cognate Words," *Journal of Theological Studies* 32 (1931) 133–53.

20 *Apocalypse of Adam* 79.15; *Apocalypse of Paul* 19.5; *Apocalypse of Peter* 75.4; 82.23; *Authoritative Teaching* 34.28; *Concept of Our Great Power* 42.17; *Holy Book of the Great Invisible Spirit* 57.10–20; 59.25; *Paraphrase of Shem* 21.26, 36; 22.7, 25; 23.9, 16; 24.7; 25.9, 19, 22, 26, 29; 27.24; 28.7, 15; 29.10, 17; 30.1, 8, 23, 32; 31.16, 19; 32.6, 16; 34.5; 35.15, 19; 36.27; 37.21; 40.26; 44.6, 15, 31; 45.17, 23; *Testimony of Truth* 29.17; 42.25; *Trimorphic Protennoia* 35.17; 40.5; 41.6; *Zostrianos* 43.12.

21 *Holy Book of the Great Invisible Spirit* 57.10–20.

22 *Gospel of Judas* 46.17.

23 Kasser *et al.*, *The Gospel of Judas*, 32. Karen King likewise translates this "separated me *for*" rather than "separated me *from*": Pagels and King, *Reading Judas*, 116.

24 Bentley Layton, *A Coptic Grammar*, 2nd edn. (Wiesbaden: Harrassowitz Verlag, 2004), sec. 181.

25 W. E. Crum, *A Coptic Dictionary* (Oxford: Clarendon Press, 1939), 271b–272a.

26 *Gospel of Judas* 46.5–7.

27 Kasser *et al.*, *The Gospel of Judas*, 32. Karen King's translation reads, "Judas said, 'Teacher, surely the rulers are not subject to my seed?' "

This translation has transposed the Coptic subject of the verb, "my seed", and the object of the verb, "the rulers." It also wrongly follows the interrogative form of the National Geographic team's translation. See Pagels and King, *Reading Judas*, 116.

28 *Gospel of Judas* 46.6–7.
29 Layton, *A Coptic Grammar*, section 240.
30 *Gospel of Judas* 46.7–14.
31 *Gospel of Judas* 46.25.
32 Rodolphe Kassen and Gregor Wurst, *The Gospel of Judas, Critical Edition: Together with the Letter of Peter to Philip, James and a Book of Allogenes from Codex Tchacos* (Washington D.C.: National Geographic, 2007).
33 Pagels and King, *Reading Judas*, 116, 142–3.
34 Bart D. Ehrman, *The Lost Gospel of Judas Iscariot: A New Look at Betrayer and Betrayed* (Oxford: Oxford University Press, 2006), 93.
35 *Gospel of Judas* 56.18–19.
36 Kasser *et al.*, *The Gospel of Judas*, 43. Karen King's translation follows the lead of National Geographic, but with an even more superlative force: "you will *surpass* them all." See Pagels and King, *Reading Judas*, 121.
37 Layton, *A Coptic Grammar*, sec. 183.
38 *Gospel of Judas* 56.17.
39 *Gospel of Judas* 56.23; Kasser *et al.*, *The Gospel of Judas*, 43.
40 Crum, *A Coptic Dictionary*, 759a.
41 Kasser *et al.*, *The Gospel of Judas*, 80, 84, 90–1, 97–101, 139, 164–5, 167.
42 *Gospel of Judas* 44.21; 35.23–27; 46.8–13, 5–7, 15–18, 24–47.1; 45.12–46.2; 56.18–19.

Chapter 4: The *Gospel of Judas* in English Translation

1 Andrew Cockburn, "The Judas Gospel," *National Geographic*, May 2006, 94.
2 James M. Robinson, *The Secrets of Judas: The Story of the Misunderstood Disciple and His Lost Gospel* (San Francisco: Harper, 2006), 117–20; Herbert Krosney, *The Lost Gospel: The Quest for the Gospel of Judas Iscariot* (Washington, DC: National Geographic, 2006), 9–12.
3 A list of the whereabouts of these fragments is kept by Ernest A. Muro, Jr. on the World Wide Web. See < www.breadofangels.com/geneva1983/exodus/index.html >.
4 D. A. Desilva and M. P. Adams, "Seven Papyrus Fragments of a Greek Manuscript of Exodus," *Vetus Testamentum* 56 (2006), 143–70.
5 Robinson, *The Secrets of Judas*, 117–20.
6 Krosney, *The Lost Gospel*, 226–7, reports that both sections of the treatise will be published by A. Jones and R. Bagnall in 2008.

 7 The National Geographic team has translated this "as a child," from a
    Boharic word that is not quite the form that we have in the Coptic
    Gospel of Judas (see Crum, *A Coptic Dictionary*, 631a-b). They also
    suggest an alternative in Boharic that means "as an apparition." But
    neither of these Boharic translations is likely. Instead, the word is a
    common Sahidic word, *htor*, meaning "necessity" (ibid., 726b–727a). Its
    literal translation is "in necessity." In agreement with John Turner, I
    have tried to render it more idiomatically in English, "when necessary."
    For Turner's translation, see his article, "The Place of the *Gospel of
    Judas* in Sethian Tradition," in Madeleine Scopello (ed.), *L'Évangile de
    Judas: le contexte historique et littéraire d'un nouvel apocryphe/The
    Gospel of Judas: The Historical and Literary Context of a New
    Apocryphal Text* (Leiden: Brill, forthcoming).
 8 Because of the fragmentary nature of the manuscript, it cannot be
    certain that these lines are spoken by Jesus. But given the fact that Jesus
    and Judas are in dialogue in this section, it appears that Jesus has just
    finished speaking here. Then Judas asks him a question. So I have taken
    the liberty of marking the end of this line with a closing quotation mark,
    fairly confident that this sentence is spoken by Jesus.
 9 Or: be controlled by. The normal use of the Coptic verb, *hypotasse*, can
    be peculiar, its active form often used to indicate the passive in Coptic
    when it is followed by a dative, which we may have here if we read *n-* as
    na- rather than the direct object marker *n-* as *mmo-* (cf. *Apocryphon of
    John* III. 11.12; Luke 10.17, 20 [Sahidic]; Romans 8.7 [Sahidic]).
10 National Geographic has "El." But as John Turner has argued, the
    mythology would suggest the reconstruction "Eleleth," which I follow
    here. See his "The Place of the *Gospel of Judas* in Sethian Tradition," in
    Madeleine Scopello (ed.), *L'Évangile de Judas: le contexte historique et
    littéraire d'un nouvel apocryphe/The Gospel of Judas: The Historical and
    Literary Context of a New Apocryphal* (Leiden: Brill, forthcoming).
11 Due to the fragmentary nature of the manuscript, it is not clear exactly
    where the speech of the Archons ends. It appears to end somewhere on
    55.2 or 55.3, because what follows is the statement that their speech was
    accomplished when the five angels came into existence.
12 I am entirely dependent on John Turner's reconstruction of 52.5–8: see
    note 11. I discuss this reconstruction in detail in Chapter 6, in the
    section titled "The Thirteenth Demon."

Chapter 5: Judas the Confessor

 1 *Gospel of Judas* 33.1–18.
 2 *Gospel of Judas* 33.19–21. This reconstructrion follows that of John
    Turner. For Turner's translation, see his article, "The Place of the
    Gospel of Judas in Sethian Tradition," in Madeleine Scopello (ed.),

L'Évangile de Judas: le contexte historique et littéraire d'un nouvel apocryphe/The Gospel of Judas: The Historical and Literary Context of a New Apocryphal Text (Leiden: Brill, forthcoming).

3 *Gospel of Judas* 33.26–35.1.

4 Mark 8.27–30.

5 Matthew 16.13–16.

6 Luke 9.18–20.

7 *Gospel of Thomas* 13.

8 John 10.30–33.

9 *Gospel of Judas* 34.11–13.

10 *Gospel of Judas* 34.13–18.

11 *Gospel of Judas* 35.10–14.

12 Jarl Fossum, *The Name of God and the Angel of the Lord*, Wissenschaftliche Untersuchungen zum Neuven Testament 36 (Tübingen: Mohr Siebeck, 1985), 55–8, 120–4, 139–41.

13 *Gospel of Judas* 35.14–21.

14 April D. DeConick, *The Original Gospel of Thomas in Translation, With a Commentary and New English Translation of the Complete Gospel*, Library of New Testament Studies 287 (London: 2006, T&T Clark), 84–5.

15 *Three Steles of Seth* 125.10.

16 Tertullian, *Prescription Against Heretics* 22.1–23.1.

17 Ibid. 22.3–7.

18 Ibid. 20.2–7.

19 Irenaeus, *Against Heresies* 1.23.1–4.

20 Ibid. 1.28.1; 1.29.1.

21 Mark 9.15–19.

22 Mark 3.13–19.

23 Mark 4.10–20.

24 Mark 4.37–41.

25 Mark 6.52.

26 Mark 8.15–21.

27 Mark 8.31–33.

28 Mark 9.15–19.

29 Mark 9.33–35.

30 Mark 10.35–45.

31 Mark 10.13–14.

32 Mark 14.50.

33 Mark 14.54–72.

34 Mark 16.14.

35 Mark 7.14–23.

36 Mark 7.24–30; 15.39.

37 Mark 10.45; cf. 8.31; 9.31; 10.33.

38 Mark 10.45.

39 Mark 8.31–33//Matthew 16.21–23.

190 NOTES

40 Mark 3.11.
41 Rodolphe Kasser, Marvin Meyer, and Gregor Wurst, *The Gospel of Judas* (Washington, DC: National Geographic, 2006), 97–8, 140; see also the immediate releases of two of the team members: Bart D. Ehrman, *The Lost Gospel of Judas Iscariot* (Oxford: Oxford University Press, 2006), 89–90; Craig A. Evans, *Fabricating Jesus: How Modern Scholars Distort the Gospels* (Downers Grove, Ill.: Intervarsity Press, 2006), 242–5.
42 Cf. Luke 22.3; John 13.26–27.

Chapter 6: Judas the Demon

1 This point is discussed in more detail in Chapter 3.
2 *Gospel of Judas* 44.21.
3 *Gospel of Judas* 46.14–24.
4 Rodolphe Kasser, Marvin Meyer, and Gregor Wurst, *The Gospel of Judas* (Washington, DC: National Geographic, 2006), 164–5.
5 *Holy Book of the Great Invisible Spirit* IV.57.10–58.25; cf. especially III.57.10–20.
6 *Holy Book of the Great Invisible Spirit* 63.19.
7 *Holy Book of the Great Invisible Spirit* 64.4.
8 *Apocalypse of Adam* 7.26–82.20.
9 *Apocalypse of Adam* 77.5–19.
10 *Apocalypse of Adam* 82.10–21.
11 *Apocalypse of Adam* 82.20–83.24.
12 *Zostrianos* 4.20–31.
13 *Gospel of Judas* 51.5–52.14.
14 I am indebted to Professor John Turner, who shared this observation with me before publishing it. This reconstruction is completely his own and will be published in his forthcoming article, "The Place of the *Gospel of Judas* in Sethian Tradition" in Madeleine Scopello (ed.), *L'Évangile de Judas: le contexte historique et littéraire d'un nouvel apocryphe/The Gospel of Judas: The Historical and Literary Context of a New Apocryphal Text* (Leiden: Brill, forthcoming).
15 Seth is called an Archon by Epiphanius, *Panarion* 26.10.1; cf. *On the Origin of the World* 117.15–18.
16 *Apocryphon of John* II.12.16; *Holy Book of the Great Invisible Spirit* III.58.10; cf. *Apocryphon of John* II.10.29–30, which probably should be reconstructed "Athoth, whom the generations call [their good one]."
17 *Gospel of Judas* 55.10.
18 *Gospel of Judas* 55.12–17.
19 *Gospel of Judas* 45.25–46.24.
20 *Gospel of Judas* 44.24–26.
21 *Gospel of Judas* 35.26–36.3; cf. Acts 1.12–14.

22 *First Apocalypse of James* 26.2–27.25.
23 *First Apocalypse of James* 36.1.3.
24 Irenaeus, *Against Heresies*, 2.20.1–2.21.1.
25 Excerpts of Theodotus 25.2.
26 *Gospel of Judas* 36.11–37.20.
27 *Gospel of Judas* 37.21–39.5.
28 *Gospel of Judas* 39.6–40.26.
29 *Gospel of Judas* 44.15–45.12.
30 *Gospel of Judas* 45.12–46.4.
31 *Gospel of Judas* 46.5–13.
32 *Gospel of Judas* 35.26–27.
33 *Gospel of Judas* 46.13–47.1.
34 *Gospel of Judas* 57.15–20.
35 *Gospel of Judas* 57.23.
36 *Gospel of Judas* 51.5–17.
37 *Apocryphon of John* 10.7–20.
38 *On the Origin of the World* 106.4.
39 *Holy Book of the Invisible Spirit* 57.10–20.
40 *Gospel of Judas* 35.26–36.4.
41 *Gospel of Judas* 45.24–26.
42 *Gospel of Judas* 46.5–47.1.
43 *Gospel of Judas* 35.24–25.
44 *Gospel of Judas* 53.7–55.23.
45 *Gospel of Judas* 53.19–53.25.
46 *Gospel of Judas* 53.19–53.25.
47 Hippolytus, *Refutations* 5.10.2.
48 *Apocalypse of Adam* 85.22–31.
49 *Holy Book of the Invisible Spirit* 63.25–64.9.
50 *Holy Book of the Invisible Spirit* 66.1–9.
51 Clement of Alexandria, *Excerpts of Theodotus* 78.1–2.
52 *Gospel of Judas* 42.7–8.
53 *Gospel of Judas* 43.1–11.
54 *Gospel of Judas* 55.15–20.
55 *Gospel of Judas* 55.21–23.
56 *Gospel of Judas* 55.24–25.
57 *Gospel of Judas* 56.11–13.

Chapter 7: Judas the Sacrificer

1 *Gospel of Judas* 56.17–21.
2 *Gospel of Judas* 56.21–24.
3 Psalm 89.24; 92.10; 112.9.
4 Even though Seth is not mentioned in this treatise, I understand this text to belong to the Sethian tradition because its markers are typical of

Sethian literature: Ennoia, Sophia, Ialdabaoth and Adonaios are all present, as well as reverse exegesis typical of Sethian interpretation of the Genesis story: the story assumes the supernatural war between Ialdabaoth and the Father and the participation of certain human beings in that drama. Its connection to Sethianism was apparent to the person in the ancient world who gave this text a Sethian title.

5   *Second Treatise of the Great Seth* 50.11.

6   *Second Treatise of the Great Seth* 51.20–25.

7   *Second Treatise of the Great Seth* 51.25–52.3.

8   *Second Treatise of the Great Seth* 55.5–6.

9   *Second Treatise of the Great Seth* 55.19–20.

10 *Second Treatise of the Great Seth* 55.30–35.

11 *Second Treatise of the Great Seth* 56.10. This teaching about the crucifixion was probably Basilides' as well, a teaching I think he picked up from the Sethian Gnostics and which became perverted in the testimony of the Church Fathers to suggest that Simon and Jesus exchanged places.

12 *Melchizedek* 25.1–26.13.

13 *Second Treatise of the Great Seth* 56.20.

14 *Second Treatise of the Great Seth* 58.25–59.18.

15 *Second Treatise of the Great Seth* 58.28–59.14.

16 *Apocalypse of Peter* 82.5–83.10.

17 *Concept of Our Great Power* 42.1–8.

18 *Concept of Our Great Power* 41.14–42.11.

19 *Gospel of Judas* 46.6–7.

20 *Gospel of Judas* 56.17–21.

21 *Gospel of Judas* 56.11–13; 39.18–40.1.

22 *Gospel of Judas* 40.18–40.25.

23 *Gospel of Judas* 33.26–34.6.

24 *Gospel of Judas* 34.6–11.

25 Ignatius, *Letter to the Philippians* 4.

26 Irenaeus, *Against Heresies* 5.32.

27 Papias as quoted by Theophylact in the *Ante-Nicene Fathers*, vol. 1 (repr. Grand Rapids: Eerdmans, 1987), 153.

28 Origen, *Against Celsus* 12.

29 Ibid. 20.

30 Tertullian, *Against Marcion* 2.28.2; 4.41.1.

31 Ibid. 4.41.1.

32 Tertullian, *Treatise on the Soul* 11.

33 Tertullian, *Against Marcion* 3.7.

34 Ibid. 5.7.

35 Origen, *On First Principles* 3.2; *Commentary on John* 10.30.

36 Origen, *Commentary on Matthew* 11.9.

37 Cf. Mark 10.45; Matthew 20.28; Romans 3.24; 8.23; 1 Timothy 2.5–6.

38 Justin Martyr, *Dialogue with Trypho* 134.5.
39 Ibid. 95.2–3.
40 Irenaeus, *Against Heresies* 5.1.1.
41 Origen, *Commentary on Matthew* 13.8.
42 Ibid.
43 Ibid. 13.9.
44 Ibid. 12.40.
45 Alister E. McGrath, *Christian Theology: An Introduction* (Oxford: Blackwell, 2001), 415–16.

Chapter 8: An Ancient Gnostic Parody

1 *Gospel of Judas* 57.9.

Epilogue

1 Interview with Andrew Lloyd Webber, *Christian Century*, March 18–25, 1987, 272–6.

Index of Authors

Adams, M.P. 187

Barnstone, W. 162
Bauer, W. 158
Bettenson, H. 158

Cameron, R. 160
Cockburn, A. 156, 187
Couliano, I.P. 162
Crum, W.E. 186–8

Darby, F. 47
DeConick, A.D. 189
Denzy, N. 160
Desilva, D.A. 187
Dunderberg, I. 160

Ehrman, B.D. 46, 57–8, 156–9,
    183–7, 190
Elliott, J.K. 160
Emmel, S. xviii, xix, 64, 183
Evans, C.A. 156, 160, 183, 190

Filoramo, G. 162
Foerster, W. 162, 186
Fossum, J. 189
Frenschkowski, M. 184
Funk, W.-P. xvii

Gathercole, S. 156
Gaudard, F. xvii, 156, 183
Greschat, K. 184

Haggmark, S.A. 159
Häkkinen, S. 160
Head, P. 156
Heath, G.L. 157
Hennecke, E. 161
Hopfner, T. 186
Hultgren, A. 159

Jonas, H. 162
Jones, F.S. 160

Kasser, R. xvii, 47, 62, 156, 183,
    185–7, 190
Klauck, H.-J. 161
King, K.L. 56, 157, 163, 183,
    186–7
Koester, H. 161
Krosney, H. 157, 184–5, 187

Lampe, P. 159
Lapham, F. 161
Layton, B. 163, 186–7
Logan, A. 164
Louth, A. 160
Lüdemann, G. 159
Luomanen, P. 159–60
Luttikhuizen, G.P. 160

Marjanen, A. 159–60
Markschies, C. 164
May, G. 184
McGrath, A.E. 193

Meyer, M. xvii, xx, 46–7, 56, 156–7, 162, 164, 183, 185–7, 190
Moreschini, C. 161
Muro, E.A. 187
Myllykoski, M. 160

Norelli, E. 161

Owen, E.C.E. 186

Pagels, E. 186
Painchaud, L. xix, 148
Pearson, B. 160, 164
Perrin, N. 157
Petersen, W. 160
Pétrement, S. 165
Porter, S. 157

Räisänen, H. 160

Robinson, J.M. 157, 165, 187
Roukema, R, 165
Rudolph, K. 165

Schneemelcher, W. 161
Scopello, M. xviii, 183, 185, 188, 190
Senior, D. 183
Staniforth, M. 160

Tabbernee, W. 184
Thomassen, E. xx, 165
Turner, J. xviii, xix, xx, 166, 185, 188, 190

Williams, M. 160, 166
Wright, N.T. 158
Wurst, G. xvii, 47, 56, 156, 183, 185–7, 190

Index of References

OLD TESTAMENT
Genesis
1–6   168
1.26   30
3.8   184
3.9   184
6.3   15
8.1-5   15
14.18   170
16.7-13   184
32.20   184

Exodus
3.1-6   184
33.20   184

Deuteronomy
5.9   184
6.15   184
32.39   184

Psalms
89.24   191
92.10   191
109.1   134
110.4   170
112.9   191

Proverbs
3.16   185
3.18   185
8.22   185
8.30   185

Isaiah
43.10-11   184
45.5-6   184
45.7   184
45.18   184
45.22   184
46.9   184
47.8   184
47.10   184

Hosea
13.4   185

Joel
2.27   185

Wisdom of Solomon
7.22-26   185
7.27   185
8.3-4   185
9.9   185
9.10   185
10.1-2   185

OLD TESTAMENT
APOCRYPHA AND
PSEUDEPIGRAPHA
Wisdom of Ben Sirach
1.9   185
24.1-7   185
24.9   185

Baruch
3.29   185

NEW TESTAMENT
Matthew
16.13-16   189
16.21-23   189
20.28   192

Mark
1.34   107
3.11   107, 190
3.13-19   189
4.10-20   189
4.37-41   189
5.6-7   107
6.52   189
7.14-23   189
7.24-30   189
8.15-21   189
8.27-30   189
8.31-33   107, 189
8.31   189
9.15-19   189
9.31   189
9.33-35   189
10.13-14   189
10.33   189
10.35-45   189
10.45   189, 192
14   143
14.50   189
14.54-72   189
15.39   189
16.14   189

Luke
9.18-20   189
10.17   188
10.20   188
22.3   190

John
10   97
10.30-33   189

13.26-27   190
14.16   184
16.13   184

Acts
1.12-14   190
2.17-18   184
8.9-24   102
13.1   184
17.23   134
21.8-10   184

Romans
3.24   192
8.23   192

1 Corinthians
11.5   184
15.3-5   184

1 Timothy
2.5-6   192

Revelation
14.3-5   184
21.1-4   184
21.10   184

NEW TESTAMENT
APOCRYPHA, NAG
HAMMADI CODICES AND
CODEX TCHACOS
Apocalypse of Adam
7.26–82.20   190
77.5-19   190
79.15   186
82.10-21   190
82.20–83.24   190
85.22-31   191

Apocalypse of Paul
19.5   186

Apocalypse of Peter
75.4   186
82.5–83.10   192
82.23   186

Apocryphon of John
4.20–5.10   185
9.25–10.20   185
10.7-20   191
29.23-25   185
II.10.29-30   190
II.12.16   190
III.11-12   188

Authoritative Teaching
34.28   186

Concept of Our Great Power
41.14–42.11   192
42.1-8   192
42.17   186

First Apocalypse of James
26.2–27.25   191
36.1.3   191

Gospel of Judas
33   140
33.1-18   188
33.19-21   188
33.26–35.1   189
34   140
34.11-13   189
34.13-18   189
35   140
35.7   186
35.10-14   189
35.14-21   189
35.17-20   185
35.23-27   187
35.24-25   191
35.26–36.4   191

35.26–36.3   190
35.26-27   191
36   141
36.11–37.20   191
37   141
37.19   186
37.21–39.5   191
38   141
39   141
39.6–40.26   191
40   141
41–44   141
42   123
42.7-8   191
43   123
43.1-11   191
43.19   186
44–45   142
44.15–45.12   191
44.21   186, 187, 190
44.24-26   190
45.12–46.4   191
45.12–46.2   187
45.24-26   191
45.25–46.24   190
46   51, 142
46.5–47.1   191
46.5-13   191
46.5-7   186, 187
46.6-7   187
46.7-14   187
46.8-13   187
46.13–47.1   191
46.14-24   190
46.15-18   187
46.17   186
46.18–47.1   120
46.23–47.1   57
46.24–47.1   187
46.24   54, 55
46.25   54, 55, 187
47–55   142

47.1–55.9   120
47.1   55, 56
47.5-13   185
47.9   186
47.14-21   185
47.21–51.1   185
49.12   186
49.16   186
51.1   xx
51.2-3   185
51.4–52.14   185
51.5–52.14   190
51.5-17   191
52.5-8   xix, 188
52.5   185
52.15–55.21   185
53.7–55.23   191
53.17   186
53.19–53.25   191
53.20   186
53.23   186
53.25   186
54.5   186
54.8-13   185
55   123
55.2   188
55.3   188
55.10-20   121
55.10   190
55.12-17   190
55.15-20   191
55.21-23   191
55.24-25   191
56   57, 59, 123, 143
56.11-13   191
56.17-21   xix, 191
56.17   187
56.18-19   187
56.21-24   191
56.23   187
57   143
57.9   193

57.15-20   191
57.23   191
58   143

Gospel of Thomas
13   189

Gospel of Philip
52.21-25   184

*Holy Book of the Great Invisible
Spirit*
57.10-20   186, 191
59.25   186
63.19   190
63.25–64.9   191
64.4   190
66.1-9   191
III.57.10-20   190
III.58.10   190
IV.57.10-58.25   190

Melchizedek
25.1–26.13   192

On the Origin of the World
106.4   191
117.15-18   190

Paraphrase of Shem
21.26   186
21.36   186
22.7   186
22.25   186
23.9   186
23.16   186
24.7   186
25.9   186
25.19   186
25.22   186
25.26   186
25.29   186

27.24   186
28.7   186
28.15   186
29.10   186
29.17   186
30.1   186
30.8   186
30.23   186
30.32   186
31.16   186
31.19   186
32.6   186
32.16   186
34.5   186
35.15   186
35.19   186
36.27   186
37.21   186
40.26   186
44.6   186
44.15   186
44.31   186
45.17   186
45.23   186

Second Treatise of the Great Seth
50.11   192
51.20-25   192
51.25–52.3   192
55.5-6   192
55.19-20   192
55.30-35   192
56.10   192
56.20   192
58.25–59.18   192
58.28–59.14   192

Testimony of Truth
29.17   186
42.25   186

Three Steles of Seth
125.10   189

Trimorphic Protennoia
35.17   186
40.5   186
41.6   186

Zostrianos
4.20-31   190
43.12   186

PATRISTIC LITERATURE
Clement of Alexandria
Excerpts of Theodotus
25.2   191
78.1-2   191
Miscellanies
1.145-1.146.4   184

Cyril of Jerusalem
Catachesis
18.26   184

Epiphanius
Medicine Chest
38.1.2-5   176
38.3.1-5   176
Panarion
26.10.1   190
40.7.6   172

Justin Martyr
1 Apology
26   184
Dialogue With Trypho
47   184
95.2-3   193
134.5   193
Hippolytus
Refutations
5.10.2   191

Ignatius
Letter to the Philippians
4   192

Irenaeus
Against Heresies
1.29-30   167, 184
1.10.1   184
1.10.2-3   184
1.23.1-4   189
1.28.1   189
1.29.1   189
1.31.1   174, 183
2.20.1-2.21.1   191
5.1.1   193
5.32   192

Origen
Against Celsus
12   192
20   192
Commentary on John
10.30   192
Commentary on Matthew
11.9   192
12.40   193
13.8   193
13.9   193
On First Principles
3.2   192

Pseudo-Tertullian
Against All Heresies
2.5-6   175

Tertullian
Against Marcion
3.7   192
5.7   192
5.19   184
2.28.2   192
4.41.1   192
Against Praxeas
1   184
Prescription Against Heretics
20.2-7   189
22.1–23.1   189
22.3-7   189
Treatise on the Soul
11   192

OTHER ANCIENT
LITERATURE
Plato
Phaedo
83d-e   186
Symposium
202e-203a   186

Porphyry
Life of Plotinus
16   171, 172